IMAGES
of America

JEKYLL ISLAND
A STATE PARK

Tyler E. Bagwell

ARCADIA
PUBLISHING

Published by Arcadia Publishing
Charleston, South Carolina

Printed in the United States of America

Library of Congress Catalog Card Number: 2001090641

For all general information contact Arcadia Publishing at:
Telephone 843-853-2070
Fax 843-853-0044
E-mail sales@arcadiapublishing.com
For customer service and orders:
Toll-Free 1-888-313-2665

Visit us on the Internet at www.arcadiapublishing.com

"Mr. Morgan died during the 2nd World War and after the war was over the directors and officers tried to open the club . . . The old 'Jekyll Island' steam ferry boat was all worn out and a new one would cost over $75,000. The cost to build a causeway to the island was prohibitive . . . The roads were all covered with palmetto roots which had made a shambles of the principal roads. The club house and the power house needed extensive repairs. While the directors and officers were discussing these problems as well as the problem of securing some new members, as treasurer, I suddenly received a check from the State of Georgia for $300,000 and in their letter I was told that the state was taking over Jekyll Island as a state park . . . and that was the end of the Jekyll Island Club." This excerpt comes from a letter written in 1983 by Jekyll Island Club member Dudley H. Mills; the photograph was taken c. 1960. (Courtesy of Jekyll Island Museum.)

CONTENTS

Introduction   6

1.   The World War II Years   9

2.   A Public Playground   21

3.   The White Elephant   45

4.   Fabulous Jekyll Island   77

5.   The Most Golden of Golden Isles   115

Bibliography   127

Acknowledgments   128

INTRODUCTION

The Jekyll Island Club, proprietor of the island before the State, opened every year in early January and closed in April. In 1942 the club season ended on April 5th, and employees set about covering furniture, shuttering windows, and preparing for the next season. America's involvement in World War II, however, was increasing. Three days after the closing, a German submarine torpedoed two American tankers near Sea Island, Georgia. Cases of chicken, quarters of beef, cans of paint, and other debris from the torpedoed ships washed ashore on the north end of Jekyll. In April 1942 German spies were secretly dropped off in New York and Florida. Their eventual capture as well as the submarine attacks prompted watch and guard patrols along the Atlantic coast. Lillian Schaitberger, daughter of the 1940s island caretaker, recalls club superintendent Michel De Zutter stating that one of the captured spies had been a waiter at Jekyll. Although none of the agents are listed in the remaining Club employee records, one of the spies, George Dasch, was known to have been a waiter at several locations in New York. De Zutter also managed resorts in that area.

By late April 1942, soldiers from the 104th Infantry Division guarded the coast of Georgia. With the arrival of the 725th MP Battalion that fall, the 104th switched to protecting the mainland while the 725th guarded the islands and the Coast Guard patrolled the shoreline. The club's financial difficulties and the war meant fewer workers were on Jekyll in the off-season of 1942; those who were served under the direction of Rufus Bennett. Since club dues had not been collected past 1942, island timber-cutting operations helped produce income.

In March 1945 the Georgia Legislature passed a resolution declaring that seashore recreational facilities should be acquired. In 1946, Revenue Commissioner Melvin E. Thompson chaired a committee that visited many of the Georgia islands in search of property. Jekyll Island was selected as the best. According to a *Brunswick News* article on September 26, 1946, "The proximity of the island to the mainland, facilities already installed there, which include a golf course, swimming pool, many miles of roadways, and a large clubhouse which could be converted into a hotel, as well as the natural beauty of the island were cited by the committee as reasons for the choice of Jekyll as the most suited on the coast for a state park." The committee promoted the purchase of Jekyll, but Gov. Ellis Arnall delayed buying it. In a complicated turn of events, Gov. Melvin Thompson would eventually acquire Jekyll.

Eugene Talmadge, elected governor in 1946, died before taking office and legal confusion ensued over who should be governor. Traditionally, the situation would have called for the legislature to select the new governor from the candidates receiving the highest number of votes. But, in 1945, the position of lieutenant governor was formed, and it was declared that in the event of the governor's death, the lieutenant governor became governor. With this new position in mind, Ellis Arnall felt he should remain governor until the lieutenant governor, a position to which Melvin Thompson was elected, could be sworn into office. On the contrary, Herman Talmadge, the son of governor-elect Eugene Talmadge, believed the decision should be made by the General Assembly. Since Herman Talmadge obtained votes, he was considered a nominee for the office. In January 1947 the legislature voted Herman Talmadge the governor. Conversely, the Georgia Supreme Court ruled in March that Thompson should be governor, and Talmadge graciously stepped down from office.

On June 2, 1947 Gov. Melvin Thompson purchased Jekyll through condemnation proceedings for $675,000. Considered a bargain, the island was designated a state park. The Georgia State Parks Department took possession of the island on October 7, 1947, and by early November, repairs were made to island structures and roads. The Jekyll Island Club formally dissolved in late January 1948, and Jekyll Island State Park officially opened on March 5th of the same year. Although construction of a causeway to Jekyll was started in 1948, transportation to the island was mainly by boat until 1954.

IMAGES
of America

JEKYLL ISLAND
A STATE PARK

The sign marking the entrance of the Jekyll causeway is pictured above in the late 1950s or early 1960s. (Courtesy of the Jekyll Island Museum.)

This book is dedicated to the memories of my aunt Patsy Bagwell, my grandmother Julia Bagwell, my grandparents Ernst and Grovie Brender, and my great-grandmother Leila Lunsford. Through their stories of days past, my interest in history was sparked.

Herman Talmadge became governor of Georgia following a special gubernatorial election in the fall of 1948. Throughout his campaign, Talmadge often disparaged the acquisition of Jekyll and referred to the island as a "white elephant." In later years, Herman Talmadge stated that the purchase was an asset to Georgia. However, in early 1949 Governor Talmadge announced that Jekyll Island was bankrupting the State Parks Department. In response, the legislature passed a resolution in February 1949 calling for a committee to decide what should be done with Jekyll. Governor Talmadge stated that the committee, besides determining Jekyll's fate, would also lease the island until his term in office expired. Bids to operate Jekyll were sent in by several people, including Melvin Thompson and Sen. James Dykes, but the best proposal came from hotel entrepreneur Barney B. Whitaker.

Barney Whitaker leased the island from May 1949 to early January 1951. Although operating Jekyll became a financial burden, the Whitakers kept the island accessible to the public. In February 1950, Governor Talmadge formed the Jekyll Island State Park Authority and through a legislative act sanctioned it to develop the island into a resort. In 1950 the Jekyll Island State Park Authority made plans, following the conclusion of Whitaker's lease, to erect a drawbridge and raze many of the dilapidated buildings. The Authority, as the governing entity of Jekyll often referred to itself, adopted the Jekyll Island Club's cotton boll and seashell emblem, minus the words "The" and "Club," as the island insignia.

In 1951 a convict camp was placed on the island under the direction of Superintendent Hoke Smith. Prisoners dug drainage canals and fire breaks, built the perimeter road, cleared lots for houses and motels, and operated a sawmill. Jekyll, with few exceptions, was closed to the public from September 1951 to December 1954. The Authority adhered to the Robert and Company Master Plan while developing the island, which was dubbed a wildlife preserve in 1953.

A drawbridge was completed in 1954, and on December 11th, Jekyll Island officially re-opened to the public. During this time, Tallu Fish began operating the Rockefeller Museum, William McMath opened a building supply store, and the Dykes, Oxford, and Scarboro families leased Club-era cottages. In 1955, the Pure Oil Company constructed a service station and the clubhouse and other structures were sublet to Sen. James Dykes, who eventually offered overnight accommodations at the facilities. Some of the early families erecting homes included the Bairds, Germanos, Musgroves, and Spatolas.

Pressured to make Jekyll self-sufficient as soon as possible, the Authority was placed on the defensive in 1955. Purchase orders for repair work on the clubhouse did not go through the proper government channels. Board member J.D. Compton attempted to rectify the problems on several occasions but to no avail. Finally, having no desire to take the blame for the improprieties, Compton resigned from the Authority in September 1955. The Authority received negative publicity stemming from this situation, as well as leasing procedures and the slow pace of development in 1955 and 1956.

The Georgia Legislature restructured the Jekyll Island State Park Authority in 1957 and made all the board members elected officials of the state. By March 1957 the Authority included the attorney general, state auditor, public service commissioner, state parks department director, and secretary of state. Augustus J. Hartley, a retired assistant attorney general, took over management of the island and developed Jekyll into a first-class resort.

Local civil rights activists in the early 1960s struggled to make the island accessible to all citizens of Georgia. Dr. J. Clinton Wilkes, an island resident, challenged the notion of separate but equal facilities in 1960. By having the Black Dental Association of Georgia meet on the island, Dr. Wilkes forced the Authority to quickly build a black auditorium to accommodate the conference. In March 1963 Rev. Julius C. Hope, president of the NAACP Brunswick branch, and W.W. Law, president of the NAACP Savannah branch, visited the island with several other people and attempted to use the segregated amenities. They were denied access to the golf course, indoor swimming pool, Peppermint Land Amusement Park, and motels. A lawsuit was filed. In June 1964 it was ruled that state-operated facilities at Jekyll be integrated.

In the late 1950s and 1960s motels, homes, a convention center, and shopping centers were constructed. Two towers, with restrooms and an information booth, were built in 1958 at the causeway entrance, and in 1960, a service station was constructed on the causeway as well. In August 1960 the Glynn County Board of Education began operating a school bus to Jekyll for 36 students living on the island. Residents in 1960 organized the Jekyll Island Garden Club, and in 1967, the Jekyll Island Art Association formed. The Art Association, located since 1974 in the Goodyear Cottage, initially used the Club-era skeet shooting building to display artwork.

By 1966 the clubhouse hotel was only sporadically used for overflow accommodations and, in 1972, was no longer in operation. In the 1970s Authority employees Roger Beedle and Ken DeBellis worked on renovating the cottages in the "Millionaires Village." The club-era structures were listed in the National Register of Historic Places in 1972 and designated a National Historic Landmark in 1978. The late 1970s, however, were financially challenging for Jekyll. Three motels declared bankruptcy, temporarily closing, and restoration work in the Historic District was delayed due to lack of funding.

The 1980s and 1990s ushered in prosperity and numerous improvements to the island. In 1982, with funding from the Garden Club, bike path construction began. The clubhouse hotel was renovated by private investors and opened in December 1987. To show support for historic restoration, the Friends of Historic Jekyll Island Inc., then called the Jekyll Island Museum Associates, was organized in 1987. Today, the Historic District, under the direction of Warren Murphey and the Jekyll Island Museum, is in the best condition it has been in since the 1930s.

The Jekyll Island State Park Authority was reorganized in 1978 and again in the 1980s. Board members currently include the commissioner of the Georgia Department of Natural Resources and eight state citizens. Residential dwellings are privately owned but the property they are on is leased from the Authority until December 31, 2049. If a home is sold, the lease transfers to the new owner. Since the 1982 creation of the island parking fee, Jekyll can boast that it operates without funding from the state. In a 1970 booklet entitled *Jekyll Island's Historical Heritage*, Dorothy Gibson and Mary Griffith declared, "As the old Jekyll Island of the millionaires stood unsurpassed as a vacation retreat so does the modern Jekyll Island of today stand unsurpassed as a family vacation spot. The island has become one of the country's outstanding beach resorts offering fun, activities, and entertainment for every member of the family." Indeed, Jekyll Island has truly become the public playground Gov. Melvin E. Thompson proclaimed it would be in 1948.

Through the foresight of Gov. Melvin E. Thompson (seen here during a visit to the island *c.* 1970), Jekyll Island was secured for the enjoyment of future generations. (Courtesy of the *Florida Times-Union.*)

One

THE WORLD WAR II
YEARS

"Secretary of War [Henry L.] Stinson said today that the nation should expect attacks 'all along our coast and other places [of the United States] like the raids made by German submarines on the Netherland's Caribbean Islands of Aruba.' " This remark came from an article entitled "Stinson Warns of Attacks on Coasts of U.S." that appeared in the *Brunswick News* on February 19, 1942. The photograph above, taken on Jekyll c. 1942, is of unidentified servicemen stationed on the island during WW II. (Courtesy of Lillian Schaitberger.)

By the 1930s many staff members of the Jekyll Island Club retired or began pursuing other ways to earn income. Seen here in the early 1940s, former club employees and their children reunite at the home of building contractor George Cowman Sr. Retired club superintendent Ernest Grob is in a chair at the center of the gathering. Mr. Cowman Sr. is pictured at far left with his arm around a dog and his wife, Josephine, is standing second from the left. The couple's son George Cowman Jr. stands at the far right with his wife, Ruth, sitting in front of him. Former club mechanic Hugh Flanders (second from right) leans against the house while his wife, Roseta, a past club chambermaid, is seated in front of him. Their son Clark stands with his hand on Grob's chair. Elizabeth Lederer, a chambermaid for the Maurice family, sits on the steps second from left with her daughter Marjory, third from left. David Nielsen, son of former club carpenter Chris Nielsen, is seated in the front. (Courtesy of Nikoline Nielsen.)

Pictured here c. 1942, Karsten Anderson, a watchman for the club, and Edward Joyner, a club boat captain and engineer during the early 1940s, pose on the club wharf with a 32-pound drum fish caught while fishing from the dock. (Courtesy of Lillian Schaitberger.)

With the ending of the club's 1942 season, the off-season staff prepared to maintain the island. Supposedly, Karsten Anderson started out as the summer manager, but because of WW II, he, as well as other employees, stopped working for the club. By late summer of 1942, Rufus Bennett, pictured in front of the club steamer, c. 1942, became caretaker. Bennett was hired in 1939 as a garage mechanic but quickly filled other positions, including power plant operator and boat captain. He served as caretaker until July 6, 1946. (Courtesy of Lillian Schaitberger.)

In this c. 1942 photograph, a glimpse of the beach entrance ramp on Shell Road is visible. Island caretaker Rufus Bennett, holding his granddaughter Martha and daughter Virginia, had nine children with his wife, Clifford Matilda McIntosh. Most of the children only visited Jekyll on holidays and weekends, but their daughter Lillian, far right, lived on the island from 1941 to 1943. Daughter Bernice is on the left beside an unidentified woman. From 1940 to 1946 the Bennetts lived in the commissary building on Pier Road. (Courtesy of Lillian Schaitberger.)

Ophelia Polite, standing at right in the photograph to the left, worked on the island throughout WW II. Polite, who is listed in the 1938 club records as a chambermaid in winter and a cottage caretaker in summer, checked for leaks and moths inside the clubhouse and cottages on a monthly basis in the 1940s. Her sister Essie Spaulding, standing beside her, was employed in the late 1930s as a cook in the dining hall of the club's boarding house. Pictured below in the 1940s, Ophelia Polite serves coffee to a group of unidentified people. She also cooked meals and attended to the needs of island guests on occasion. (Both courtesy of Lillian Schaitberger.)

By autumn of 1942 the Army's 725th MP Battalion replaced the 104th Infantry in the responsibility of guarding the coastal islands. The 104th Infantry remained in Brunswick but were utilized in mainland patrols. Both detachments shared the Hercules Powder Co. base camp until the 104th Infantry was transferred from the area in late January 1943. The 725th MP Battalion consisted of two companies—A and B. Each company took turns rotating every two weeks from the base camp to the various islands. Pictured at right, James "Jim" Valentine of Company B, stands in a WW I "dough boy"–style combat uniform, c. 1942. Due to the lack of supplies during the early years of WW II, soldiers were often issued older uniforms. (Courtesy of Lillian Schaitberger.)

Harry Schaitberger, standing at the front in the c. 1942 photograph above, arrives with other servicemen of Company A to the club wharf via the *Cherokee*. Charles Howard Candler Jr., a descendent of the Coca-Cola Co. founder, donated the 52-foot *Cherokee* for use during the war. (Courtesy of Lillian Schaitberger.)

An observation tower, pictured at left c. 1942, was located near the Shell Road beach ramp. The building underneath the tower contained cots for the servicemen's use during breaks. While on watch one evening, a soldier in the 725th reputedly saw lights over the ocean's horizon. Thinking it might be an enemy submarine recharging batteries, it was reported. An air ship from the Brunswick blimp base flew over the area dropping depth charges. In the end, no enemy ships were found that night, or for that matter, at any other time while the 725th was stationed on the island. (Courtesy of Lillian Schaitberger.)

Joe Gaudiello (right) and Jim Valentine handwash and hang clothing to dry alongside the boarding house, c. 1942. Like the 104th, the 725th lived in the boarding house and prepared meals in the dining room building. Servicemen alternated cooking meals. On one occasion, John "Scotty" McPhee, a soldier in Company A of the 725th, jokingly removed the labels from the ration cans during his turn as cook. For weeks no one knew what the meal was going to be until a container was opened. (Courtesy of Lillian Schaitberger.)

The 725th enjoyed leisure activities such as swimming in the clubhouse pool, bicycle riding, and playing card games with the island caretaker's family. Harry Schaitberger, pictured here c. 1942, met and dated the caretaker's daughter Lillian while stationed on Jekyll. They would marry on May 28, 1943. The structure in the background is the commissary. (Courtesy of Lillian Schaitberger.)

Clifford Matilda Bennett, the caretaker's wife, sold soft drinks, candy, and cigarettes in the commissary building to the soldiers. Pictured below, from left to right, Henry Laudermilk of the Georgia State Guard, Pfc. ? Gilbert, Scotty McPhee, Pfc. ? McDonough, Thomas Egan, and James Boland relax on the lawn near the boarding house and commissary, c. 1942. The caretaker's daughter Lillian and granddaughter Martha are also in the photograph. Like with the 104th Infantry, servicemen of the Georgia State Guard worked as radio operators for the 725th. By late July 1943 the 725th MP Battalion received reassignment papers and were transferred from Brunswick and eventually sent to Africa and Italy. (Courtesy of Lillian Schaitberger.)

Dr. Ernest Corn, friend and physician of club member Frank Gould, sojourned on Jekyll with his family and three companions of his daughter in July 1944. The Corns, staying at the Cloister resort on Sea Island, chartered a boat and resided in Villa Marianna Cottage. The trip included touring the island, bicycling, and exploring several of the cottages. Pictured above, from left to right, Dr. Corn's wife, Polly; Florence Domingos; and Ann Corn Felton relax on the terrace of Villa Marianna, *c.* 1944. Below, Ann Corn Felton, left, and her friend Helen Birdsey Everett mount a tandem bicycle. During the war years, Frank Gould honeymooned at Jekyll with his second wife, Helen. Susan Albright Reed, the daughter of former member John J. Albright, visited briefly with her husband, Robert. (Both courtesy of Susan Corn Conway.)

Two

A PUBLIC PLAYGROUND

"The State of Georgia ordered condemnation proceedings today [June 3, 1947] to acquire Jekyll Island, near Brunswick, where a group of wealthy Easterners spent more than a million dollars in the development of an exclusive winter colony. The island will be converted into a great public beach park, according to announcement of the Georgia Property Condemnation Commission, composed of Governor M.E. Thompson, Attorney General Eugene Cook, and State Auditor B.E. Thrasher Jr." This appeared in an article entitled "Georgia to Buy Island" in the *New York Times* on June 4, 1947. (Courtesy of the Jekyll Island Museum.)

The State of Georgia took formal possession of Jekyll Island on October 7, 1947. By early November, road-grading equipment was shipped to the island and approximately 15 highway department employees worked on improving the road infrastructure. While discussion of sending a work detail of 100 to 150 convicts was contemplated, it was eventually decided to use primarily contractors and paid laborers to revitalize island buildings. For a brief time in early 1948 about 30 prisoners and 6 Board of Correction guards from Reidsville, Georgia came to the island and trimmed palmettos, cut grass, and pruned golf course vegetation. Pictured above, c. 1947, unidentified workers rebuild a section of the clubhouse porch. Below, two men paint the clubhouse, c. 1947. (Both courtesy of the Jekyll Island Museum.)

Charles T. "Charlie" Morgan, director of the Georgia State Parks Department, spent months overseeing the renovation of the island. At right, c. 1947, Morgan and H.W. Oliver, chief engineer for the State Parks Department, examine a map of Jekyll. Two unidentified men also review the drawing. Jekyll Island State Park officially opened March 5, 1948. While Harry J. Glenn Jr. was appointed park superintendent, a private contract was awarded to Thomas H. Briggs Jr. to operate the clubhouse and some of the cottages as lodging facilities. (Courtesy of the Jekyll Island Museum.)

Gov. M.E. Thompson announced that, with the purchase of Jekyll, U.S. Highway 17 would be re-routed, bridges erected over Jekyll Creek and Turtle River, and a causeway constructed to the park. In early April 1948 the Hendry Corporation from Rattlesnake, Florida, was given a contract for the dredging and initial development of the causeway. Optimistically, it was proclaimed that by May 1949 it would be possible to drive an automobile directly to the island. However, throughout 1948 and until late 1954, access to the island would remain primarily by boat. Pictured above c. 1948, the sternwheeler *Robert E. Lee* picks up supplies at the Mansfield dock in Brunswick for transport to Jekyll. (Courtesy of Jack McKinney.)

The State Parks Department granted the Brunswick Chamber of Commerce control over choosing a boat for transporting people between Brunswick and Jekyll. The *Robert E. Lee*, a sternwheeler with a large passenger capacity, was selected. Owned by Leroy Simkins of Augusta, the paddlewheel boat originally operated on the Savannah River and is seen above c. 1948. Taking nearly an hour to complete the voyage one-way, the ferry left daily from the Mansfield docks in Brunswick at 9 a.m., 1 p.m., and 5 p.m. Adult passengers were charged $1.50 for a round-trip ticket. The *Biscayne*, also owned by Simkins, made regular trips to Jekyll from St. Simons Island. (Courtesy of the Jekyll Island Museum.)

While the *Lee* retained a monopoly in 1948 on the Brunswick-Jekyll route, the St. Simons-Jekyll route had competition. By mid-June 1948, the *Neptune*, pictured above in the late 1940s, began challenging the *Biscayne*. Joe Spaulding, a former Jekyll Island Club boat captain, piloted the *Neptune*. Initially, the owner of the *Robert E. Lee* was to pay the Brunswick Chamber of Commerce $5,000 for transportation rights to Jekyll. However, the State Parks Department, fearful of negative publicity near the upcoming governor election, reneged on their agreement with the chamber. Unable to offer exclusive access to the Jekyll wharf, the chamber's original agreement with Simkins was annulled. Instead, the *Lee* was charged a fee for dock usage in Brunswick. From time to time the *Bernice*, owned by former Jekyll Island Club boat captain Ed Royall, transported park employees and guests to the island. (Courtesy of Joe Spaulding Jr.)

Pictured *c.* 1948, vacationers identified as Sigma Chi fraternity brothers exit the *Robert E. Lee.* Upon landing, people spending the night on the island could either walk or obtain a ride to the clubhouse and check-in at the front desk. Bus excursions were also available to visitors on arrival. Tourists were charged a quarter for a sightseeing tour or a dime for a one-way bus ride to the beach. Below, *c.* 1948, Parks Director Charlie Morgan welcomes guests as they board a bus at the Jekyll wharf. Jeeps were also readily available at the dock and could be rented by small groups for trips around the island. (Both courtesy of the Jekyll Island Museum.)

In 1948 Thomas H. Briggs Jr. managed the Jekyll Island State Park facilities. Briggs, a former Augusta resident and owner of a hotel in Manteom, North Carolina, signed a contract with the State Parks Department to operate the clubhouse and other structures as a hotel for $500 a month and 10 percent of net profit. To insure smooth operation of the accommodations, experienced hotel workers were hired, including staff members pictured above, c. 1948. From left to right, they are (standing) W. "Red" Weatherford (assistant manager), ? Downie (clerk), Louis Maud Bowie-McKinney (executive housekeeper), Briggs, ? Hamilton (food checker), and ? Abbott (steward); (kneeling) ? O'Donnell (clerk), ? Hamilton (assistant steward), an unidentified visitor, and Mary Grahl (stenographer). (Courtesy of Jack McKinney.)

There were approximately 90 employees on the island. Most of the workers were under the supervision of Superintendent Harry J. Glenn Jr. Job positions included a recreation director, a nurse, a police officer, lifeguards, day and night watchmen, electricians, and a maintenance crew. Pictured at left, c. 1948, state park worker James Cash converses with two children. Cash, a former club employee and nephew of club employee "Sim" Denegal, was highly knowledgeable about the island's history and natural environment. (Courtesy of the Jekyll Island Museum.)

The clubhouse was renamed the Jekyll Island Hotel and provided, along with other structures on the island, between 350 to 400 rooms for visitors. Prices ranged from $1 to $3 daily. Since most of the club furnishings were purchased by the state, the majority of bedrooms included club-era items such as brass-knobbed metal beds, antique dressers, sofas, chaise lounges, and framed steel engravings on the walls. Pictured above, c. 1948, is the southern side of the Jekyll Island Hotel. (Courtesy of the Jekyll Island Museum.)

Dot and Joe Mason, pictured c. 1948 on the Jekyll Island Hotel porch, honeymooned on the island in early May. Throughout the spring and summer several newlyweds vacationed on Jekyll, and in September, Al Scheppler, supervisor of the Jekyll State Park's laundry facility, married Brunswick resident Ouida Cook in Faith Chapel. At first, the local paper proclaimed it the first wedding held in the church; however, Katherine Clark, daughter of the club's boat captain and head housekeeper, corrected the paper by explaining that two weddings occurred at Faith Chapel in the 1910s. (Courtesy of Dot and Joe Mason.)

Unidentified guests, pictured c. 1948, enter the lobby of the Jekyll Island Hotel. By December 1948 some of the hotel's smaller furnishings and items had disappeared. One state official asserted that visitors must have taken things as souvenirs; however, several employees were released from duty due to theft accusations. (Courtesy of the Jekyll Island Museum.)

The clubhouse library was included in the sale of the island. Most of the books were identified on the spine with Jekyll Island Club labels, and some volumes included bookplates acknowledging the club member who donated the book. Pictured c. 1948, a couple from Brunswick examines a book in the library. The club also sold the state a painting of Sir Joseph Jekyll, a financial backer of the Georgia colony and island namesake, and one of the *Wanderer*, the last known ship to transport slaves to America. (Courtesy of the Jekyll Island Museum.)

A high school group from Macon, Georgia, is pictured above *c*. 1948 participating in a dance on the island. The *Atlanta Journal* reported on February 29, 1948 that over 50 graduating classes from schools across the state had made hotel reservations for the month of June. Throughout the Park's opening year, youth organizations such as the Boy Scouts and the Glynn County 4-H Club made regular excursions to the island. During December, a Jewish youth leadership group held the first young adult convention on the island. A servants annex, originally built by the club to house waiters, kitchen staff, and so forth, was designated a youth group dormitory. Visitors staying in the dormitory, dubbed Thompson Hall, were charge $1 a night. The state also declared that acreage near the ocean would be set aside for use by children and young adult groups. Below, *c*. 1948, members of Boy Scout Troop 36 from Buford, Georgia dine at the Jekyll Island Hotel. (Both courtesy of the Jekyll Island Museum.)

In the summer of 1948, Edith Russell of Atlanta and eight young adults offered theatre performances on Jekyll. The acting troupe, referred to as the Edith Russell Players, transported stage lighting, sets, and costumes to the island and presented plays six nights a week over a ten-week period. The shows varied in content from comedies to mysteries. Pictured above, c. 1948, members of the group pose on the stage of the Crook-Ye-Neck Theatre, located on the first floor of Thompson Hall. Originally a club employee annex, Thompson Hall appears below, c. 1948. The erection of an outdoor theatre was discussed in 1948, but due to financial concerns the idea was not implemented until 1971. (Both courtesy of the Jekyll Island Museum.)

On August 22, 1948, over 1,500 spectators watched the Second Annual Miss Georgia State Parks Beauty Pageant at Jekyll. Sixteen-year-old Sara Kate Chew, Miss Magnolia Springs State Park, was declared the winner. Pictured above, c. 1948, journalists photograph Chew soon after the pageant's completion. Earlier that summer each state park had chosen a young woman to represent them in the finals. The title of Miss Jekyll State Park, awarded to Jane Pitts of Glynn County, was given in a contest held on August 1st. (Courtesy of the Jekyll Island Museum.)

Joanna Paulsen (far left) presented a sterling silver platter to the Miss Georgia State Park's winner Sara Kate Chew and sterling silver pitchers to the two runners-up in the contest: Sara Thornton (second from right) and Margaret Lang (far right). Paulsen, from Keokuk, Iowa, won a vacation to Jekyll and St. Simons Island on the nationally syndicated radio program, "Queen for a Day." Sponsored by the Brunswick Chamber of Commerce, the trip was given to advertise the area. (Courtesy of the Jekyll Island Museum.)

A June 7, 1948 article in *Life Magazine* stated that of the 140 miles of shoreline along Georgia, only three miles were accessible to the public before the purchase of Jekyll. In the summer of 1948, the Thompson Brothers Co. of St. Simons Island erected a beach pavilion in the location of the Jekyll Island Club's teahouse. The new structure, costing around $60,000, included concession spaces, lockers, restrooms, and an area identified as a dance floor. The *c.* 1948 postcard above shows the ocean and sand dunes visible from Shell Road. (Postcard published by South Georgia News Agency, Waycross, Georgia.)

From mid-May to mid-August, female loggerhead turtles leave the ocean and crawl to the sandy areas of the beach. With their back flippers, they dig a hole in the sand into which as many as 125 eggs may be deposited. Weighing from 175 to 300 pounds, a loggerhead turtle will often deposit eggs several times in a season. Here, a group of spectators observe a turtle on the beach. During the 1940s, people frequently stood or rode on the backs of the turtles for recreation and turtle eggs were regularly taken for food. (Courtesy of the Jekyll Island Museum.)

Expectations of the golf course being ready by the park's official opening day were thwarted by the rooting actions of wild hogs and the lack of funds to repair the greens. Free hog hunts were offered in hopes of eradicating the animals, and between March and June 1948, 35 hogs were killed. By October 1948, under the supervision of Brunswick Country Club golf pro Tommy Wilson, the front nine holes were ready for play. Greens fees were not charged until a full-time golf pro was hired. The back nine holes of the golf course are pictured above, c. 1943. Hogs were eliminated on the island in the 1950s. (Courtesy of Caesar Pavia.)

Bicycles, available for rent at the commissary building on Pier Road, enabled guests to traverse the nearly 35 miles of shell and sand roads. State employee Mac Gignilliat, whose father owned a bicycle shop in Brunswick, rented and maintained the bikes at Jekyll. Gignilliat also rented motor scooters and operated a small store inside the commissary building. Pictured c. 1948, vacationer Dot Mason bicycles on one of the island roads. (Courtesy of Dot and Joe Mason.)

Horseback riding was available for a fee when the island first opened. But, by late July, bicycling, sightseeing buses, and jeeps were the only modes of transportation advertised. Seen above c. 1948, horseback riders stroll down the then-named River Road in the vicinity of the wharf. (Courtesy of the Jekyll Island Museum.)

Pictured c. 1948, guests spend time at the Jekyll Island Hotel swimming pool, an amenity free of charge and available to all island visitors. While state park literature in 1948 advertised Jekyll as having two swimming pools, in reality only the pool near the hotel was functional. The other pool, a vestige of Chicota Cottage, was never placed in usable shape due to lack of funding. (Courtesy of Jack McKinney)

Recreational activities on the island in 1948 included badminton, croquet, horseshoe pitching, and tennis. Movies were purportedly shown nightly on the hotel veranda. Seen above c. 1948, a group of people participates in a croquet game near the Jekyll Island Hotel. Below, from left to right, John Preston, Ann Hahr Pawley, Clifton Pawley, and Ginney DePass play tennis at one of the indoor courts. Advertisements stated that Jekyll had two indoor and several outdoor courts; however, the outdoor tennis courts were probably in too poor condition for serious play. Conversely, the indoor court located behind the Sans Souci was repaired and available for free to visitors. The other indoor court was attached to the Gould Playhouse, a structure that included a shooting range, bowling alley, and several guest rooms. (Both courtesy of the Jekyll Island Museum.)

After the defeat of M.E. Thompson in the governor's election of 1948, Jekyll Island was in a state of limbo. The new governor, Herman Talmadge, decided to appoint a committee in February 1949 to determine the long-term fate of Jekyll as well as find someone to lease the island in the interim period. To find a lessee, members of the committee accepted bids to operate the island from the spring of 1949 to January 15, 1951. Barney B. Whitaker, a highly accomplished hotel owner, was selected as the lessee from the submitted proposals. Whitaker, pictured at left in his office at the Jekyll Island Hotel, c. 1949, successfully owned and managed several hotels, including the Clarendon Hotel in Augusta, Georgia for 18 years. The terms of the Jekyll lease called for Barney Whitaker to maintain the island structures and pay the State Parks Department 20 percent of gross receipts. (Courtesy of Bob and Peg Whitaker and Mary Whitaker Bailey.)

Barney Whitaker keenly envisioned Jekyll Island as a flourishing resort with tremendous potential for the future. Although numerous obstacles would hinder Whitaker and his family, they successfully kept the island in operation throughout the lease period. The Whitaker family, pictured c. 1950 at their home in Augusta, included, from left to right, (front row) Mary Harriss and Barney Sr.; (back row) their children Robert, Mary, and Barney Jr. The leasing of the island officially began on May 10, 1949. (Courtesy of Mary Whitaker Bailey.)

The Whitaker family's 1948 Buick Sedan was shipped to the island with a fishing boat in tow. The vehicle and boat, pictured above and below c. 1949, were packed to capacity with the family's belongings. In the summer of 1949, billboards advertising Jekyll were placed on several roads and a plane hired to fly around the state with a banner proclaiming "See Beautiful Jekyll Island." On June 15, a large barbecue, complete with a band from the University of Georgia, was held on the front lawn of the clubhouse. Numerous civic organizations and politicians were invited to attend. Advertisements and a free vacation competition were also employed, and every 100th honeymooning couple spent a free night at Indian Mound Cottage. During this period, former club member Charles M. Daniels honeymooned on the island with his bride, Marjorie Ellen. (Both courtesy of Mary Whitaker Bailey.)

Mary Whitaker, seen here *c.* 1949, performed numerous jobs at the resort, including serving in the dining room, giving tours of Indian Mound Cottage, and cashiering at the souvenir booth in the hotel lobby. Since it was difficult for Mary to attend high school in Brunswick, a teacher was hired to instruct her on the island. (Courtesy of Bob and Peg Whitaker and Mary Whitaker Bailey.)

In May 1949, 25 students from Richmond Academy, an all-male school in Augusta, were hired to work on Jekyll for the summer. The young men performed tasks such as bell hopping, lifeguarding, and serving food in the dining room. Above, a *c.* 1949 musical group, possibly composed of Richmond Academy cadets, performs on the dock. (Courtesy of Mary Whitaker Bailey.)

Pictured at right c. 1949, Albert Whitaker displays a fish he caught. Albert, the younger brother of Barney Whitaker, managed the hotel kitchen while his wife, Valeria Orr, worked as the dining room hostess. Their son William, employed in the summers of 1949 and 1950, helped operate the island's power plant. The Jekyll Island Hotel, except during conventions, was utilized only in the summer months. By winter, it was closed and the Crane Cottage became the main structure accommodating guests. The Whitakers, as the Jekyll lease contract required, never sold alcohol on the island. However, according to a former employee and Richmond Academy cadet, a man working on Jekyll who owned an airplane occasionally flew over bottles of liquor to sell privately to vacationers. (Courtesy of Mary Whitaker Bailey.)

State Trooper Dudley W. Gay, at left c. 1949, policed the island and lived with his wife, Nell, and their four children in the Crane Cottage. During the winter of 1950 the family made plans to move to the Clark Cottage, a home built in 1901 for Jekyll Island Club employees James and Minnie Clark. A refrigerator, several appliances, and most of their clothing were relocated to the dwelling. Unfortunately, before the move an electrical fire burned the home to the ground on February 9, 1950. The Dudleys' possessions were completely destroyed, along with numerous pieces of club-era furniture. Another fire occurred June 18, 1950 at the Gould Playhouse. The Playhouse, leased to Nell Gay and operated as a recreation hall, was discovered burning around midnight. Guests and employees attempted to extinguish the fire, but only the tennis court was saved. That evening, prior to the fire, movies were shown outdoors adjacent the structure and the equipment stored afterwards inside the Gould Playhouse. Trooper Gay transferred to Americus, Georgia in late August 1950. (Courtesy of Mary Whitaker Bailey.)

In the summer of 1949, Margaret Anne "Peg" Rodgers, vacationing with her Sunday school class from McDonough Baptist Church, made the acquaintance of Robert "Bob" Harriss Whitaker. Whitaker obtained her address from the hotel register and the two began corresponding. They would eventually marry on November 27, 1952. Pictured c. 1950, Bob Whitaker and Peg Rodgers pose on the entrance steps of the Jekyll Island Hotel. Bob and his older brother Barney B. Whitaker Jr. performed numerous jobs on the island including the operation of the snack bar adjacent the hotel dining room, rental of fishing equipment, maintenance of the swimming pool, and unloading of supplies at the wharf. Their mother, Mary Whitaker, was in charge of the housekeeping staff. (Courtesy Bob and Peg Whitaker.)

Barney and Mary Whitaker are pictured above on the Jekyll wharf, c. 1949. The Whitakers lost between $25,000 and $30,000 keeping the island open to the public. While at times Jekyll was busy with visitors and conventions, the number of people vacationing there did not compare to the 1948 summer. At the time of the lease signing, it was predicted that by the spring of 1950 the causeway would be completed and a dock placed along the road to reduce travel time to the island. These results never materialized. After completing the Jekyll lease, the Whitakers returned to Augusta and opened the Clarendon Hotel and a cafeteria named the B&W. By 1952 the cafeteria was a $200,000-a-year operation (Courtesy of Bob and Peg Whitaker.)

Sand dunes—some as high as 40 feet—were bulldozed flat along a portion of the island's ocean side by 1953. The Authority, not realizing at the time the importance of dunes to an island ecosystem, wanted a view of the ocean from the perimeter road. The sand from the dunes was used to increase the size of the Jekyll Creek Bridge earthen embankment, to fill in low places on the two-entranceway roads, and to build a road from the entranceway to the "Village," the name given to the clubhouse and cottages in early Authority meeting minutes. Topsoil from the back nine greens of the golf course was placed along the edges of various roads. Pictured c. 1957, bulldozers and tractors are seen south of the beach pavilion and bathhouse. (Courtesy of the Jekyll Island Museum.)

By early 1952 an island sawmill was processing cut logs produced in the construction of roads and the clearing of house lots. The Glynn County Realty Board in October 1954 evaluated 440 lots on Jekyll and estimated their market value to be from $3,000 to $8,000. It was determined that the yearly rental fee for a house lot would range from $100 to $400. Seen above c. 1957, a sign states, "This lot for lease $360 per year." House lots were arranged into subdivisions with names such as Jekyll Beach, Oak Grove, Palmetto, Plantation, and Pinegrove. Although lot-leasing advertisements were placed in several newspapers, by December 1954 only 126 lots out of the 500 available had been leased. (Courtesy of the Jekyll Island Museum.)

While plans were made in 1948 to build a bridge to the island, it was not until 1952 that construction began. The causeway, on the other hand, was finished by late 1950. A bridge, erected by Industrial Construction Co., was completed in November 1954. It was decided that the island would officially re-open to the public December 11th and a large ceremony was planned. Pictured *c.* 1954, Gov. Herman Talmadge and Gov.-Elect Marvin Griffin dedicate the bridge during the ceremony. Following the ribbon cutting at the bridge, an entrance marker honoring the Authority was dedicated. Numerous politicians and event attendees then gathered on the main porch of the clubhouse. Bunting and flags decorated the veranda, blimps flew overhead, bands performed, and speeches were given praising Jekyll. (Courtesy of the Jekyll Island Museum.)

A state audit determined that the Jekyll Creek drawbridge, seen in the 1960s, cost $917,840.12 to build. To help reimburse the bridge construction, automobiles were initially charged a fee of 50¢ at a tollbooth located on the bridge. Bridge tenders were hired to operate the bridge lift span, and with prisoners still on the island, were deputized and given the authority to search vehicles. The convict camp was disbanded in late December 1955. Acme Construction Co., owned by Sen. James "Jimmy" Dykes, was given a contract to surface all of the island roads, and by February 1955, paving of the perimeter road was completed. (Courtesy of the Jekyll Island Museum.)

It was declared as early as 1947 that Indian Mound Cottage, a home once owned by Standard Oil executive William Rockefeller, would be a museum. But, it was not until Tallu Fish entered the picture in 1954 that this proclamation could be considered true. On November 22, 1954 Tallu Fish, a recent widow, proposed to the Jekyll Island State Park Authority that she would act as a curator and publicist for the State Park. The Authority, familiar with her credentials, accepted her offer that day under the condition that Indian Mound Cottage be open to the public by December 11, 1954. Pictured c. 1956, a sign directs visitors to Indian Mound Cottage. (Courtesy of the Jekyll Island Museum.)

Tallu Fish, originally from Waycross, Georgia, held a degree in journalism from Brenau College. She was the former editor of the *Democratic Women's Journal* of Kentucky and had written columns for several newspapers, including the *Louisville Courier-Journal*. While living on the island, Fish wrote articles about Jekyll and authored books about the region including the 1959 *Once Upon an Island, The Story of Fabulous Jekyll Island*, the 1963 *Sidney Lanier, America's Sweet Singer of Songs*, and the 1967 *A Pretty Kettle of Fish, Jekyll Island Seafood Cookery*. In 1955 she was instrumental in having scenes from the movie *A View from Pompey's Head* filmed on Jekyll. Pictured here in the 1950s or early 1960s, Fish sits in the "Wishing Chair." Realizing the struggle of obtaining money for historic preservation, Fish ingeniously enticed visitors to the museum with a story she created about an ornately decorated chair that when set upon granted wishes. (Courtesy of Tallu Scott.)

The Jekyll Island Museum was located in the main rooms of Indian Mound Cottage, seen above in the 1950s or 1960s. The home featured items such as club-era furniture, a taxidermy display, and a pottery exhibit consisting of clubhouse chamber pots, pitchers, and bowls. From late 1954 to 1963, Tallu Fish resided in the servant's area of the cottage. Visitors bought tickets—25¢ for adults and 15¢ for children—in the hallway. Souvenir items such as straw hats, children's activity books, and sand dollars were also available for purchase. Fish paid children living on the island a penny for every sand dollar they brought her. If they were already bleached she offered 3¢ instead. Below, several grandchildren of Tallu Fish investigate the souvenir items for sale at the museum. The club-era table resembles the same table used in 1915 by AT&T president and club member Theodore Vail during the opening ceremony of the first transcontinental telephone line. (Both courtesy of Tallu Scott.)

The lease for the beach pavilions stipulated that lifeguard protection be available for ocean swimmers and that Coca-Cola would be sold for 5¢. The White Beach House, pictured above and below in the 1950s, included dressing rooms and lockers. Concession stands offered floats, umbrellas, and other items for rental or sale to tourists. Around 1956 a restaurant was built on the side of the structure opposite the changing rooms. The Jekyll Island Hotel Corporation operated the facility until 1963. (Both courtesy of the Jekyll Island Museum.)

In 1950, black community leaders from Brunswick requested a section of Jekyll for use by people of color. The Jekyll Island State Park Authority concurred and invited a local committee, which included Brunswick business owner Wendell Holmes and Brunswick Citizens Civic League chair S.G. Dent, to inspect the southern region of the island. In 1952, Savannah officials also inquired about the development. A beach pavilion for blacks, pictured above in the 1950s, opened on the south end of Jekyll on September 24, 1955. Called the Negro Beach House, the structure was one of only a few places in the South where African-descent Americans could visit the beach during segregation. (Courtesy of the Jekyll Island Museum.)

A dedication ceremony took place at the Negro Beach House on September 24, 1955. Jimmy Dykes, lessee of the structure, paid the island tolls for all attending the event. Orchestrated by Joe M. Atkinson, an official from Selden Recreational Park in Brunswick, the ceremony involved musical entertainment by the Risley School band and speeches from Rev. J.F. Mann and State Teachers Association president Luscious Bacote. Authority board members and community leaders such as grocery store owner Joseph Carmouche and funeral parlor director Wendell Holmes attended. The Negro Beach House, seen here in the 1950s, included dressing rooms, a concession stand, and a covered picnic area. (Courtesy of the Jekyll Island Museum.)

An area adjacent the Negro Beach House was cleared for the construction of a motel, and 40 house lots were staked and available for lease. Selden Park official Joe Atkinson submitted the first proposal for the erection of a motel and restaurant. The Authority also announced that a golf course and a shopping center would be built in the region. Pictured in the late 1950s, unidentified women pose near the Negro Beach House. (Courtesy of the Jekyll Island Museum.)

Vacationers in the 1950s stroll along the water's edge near the Negro Beach House. In 1958, Governor Griffin, while on a hunting trip in Canada, offered the survivors of a mineshaft collapse in Nova Scotia a free six-day Jekyll vacation. The goodwill gesture was almost refused when the miners discovered that Georgia was segregated. One of the miners, Maurice Ruddick, was of African descent. The Ruddick family and their host, Dr. W.K. Payne, president of Savannah State College, resided in trailers placed in the Negro Beach House parking lot. While Ruddick said the area was beautiful, he stated in a *Florida Times-Union* article on November 29, 1958 that he "wasn't pleased with anything that keeps people apart—it is something out of the past." (Courtesy of the Jekyll Island Museum.)

The Authority discussed renovating the clubhouse in June 1952 but decided to wait until it was rented. After advertising several times in 1954, the Jekyll Island Hotel Corporation leased the structure in 1955. The corporation, headed by Sen. Jimmy Dykes, signed a 32-year lease that would be evaluated after six years for price increases. The lease included Crane Cottage, Sans Souci, a servant's dormitory, the indoor tennis court, and two beach pavilions. Clubhouse renovations included new bathroom fixtures and the removal of the main staircase in order to install an elevator. Seen above in the 1950s, a then newly-built enclosed stairwell is discerned adjacent the tower. (Courtesy of the Jekyll Island Museum.)

By the spring of 1956, the Crane Cottage was operated as a hotel, the Sans Souci housed employees, and the indoor tennis court became a meeting space for conventions. The clubhouse, renamed the Jekyll Island Hotel, opened on December 28, 1956, and from 1957 to 1961, dances were held there on Saturdays. For $3.50 per person, couples enjoyed dinner and dancing that lasted until 1 a.m. Pictured above, c. 1956, an ensemble, possibly Sammy Middleton and his Moon-Glow orchestra, performs. (Courtesy of the Jekyll Island Museum.)

The Jekyll Island Hotel was decorated with a mixture of modern furnishings and original club-era items. In the 1950s picture above is the hotel check-in area and lobby; the 1950s picture below shows one of the chambers on the main floor. During the summer of 1956 Jimmy Dykes received criticism because companies owned or co-owned by him held the majority of business leases on the island. Some newspapers began referring to Jekyll as "Dykes Island." His applications for publicly advertised leases, however, were often the only ones received by the Authority. On August 30, 1956, Dykes proposed re-leasing the hotel properties to anyone agreeing to the same lease conditions as well as willing to reimburse his company the estimated $182,000 invested. No one accepted his offer. The Jekyll Island Hotel Corporation retained Crane Cottage until 1960 and the clubhouse until 1961. By 1963, all of the leased structures were turned back over to the Authority; the lack of business was attributed to the erection of oceanside motels. (Both courtesy of the Atlanta History Center.)

In June 1952 the Authority decided that the region around the du Bignon cemetery, pictured above in the 1950s, would not be developed. Instead, the area would become an historical park site. Near the cemetery stood the tabby remains of the Horton House, seen below c. 1960. Maj. William Horton, an officer under Georgia colony founder Gen. James Oglethorpe, initially constructed a wooden house in the vicinity in 1736. Spanish soldiers burned it in 1742, and a tabby home was erected in its place. In the early 1800s Christophe Poulain du Bignon, then proprietor of the island, lived in the Horton home and operated a plantation on Jekyll. In 1898 members of the Jekyll Island Club erected a gated wall around the cemetery and repair work was performed on the house to help preserve it. (Both courtesy of the Jekyll Island Museum.)

A section of the beachfront lots are seen above in the late 1950s. In April 1955, only two houses were under construction. A.D. Holland, a Georgia Tech professor, built the first home on a leased lot. The Authority, under pressure to make Jekyll financially self-sufficient, hoped to achieve this goal by earning revenue from lot leases. Finding lessees, however, became a challenge. Perhaps people were initially uncomfortable with the idea of renting a lot. To be sure, Governor Griffin's statements in 1955 and 1956 encouraging the sale of Jekyll did not help the matter. In 1961 approximately 97 homes were on the island. By 1964 this number had increased to 326. In the 1960s the Authority declared that limiting houses on the island was necessary to preserve Jekyll's ecological splendor. (Courtesy of the Jekyll Island Museum.)

In the 1950s Norbert Overstolz, pictured in front of his home in the 1950s, operated a real estate business on Jekyll. Norbert and his wife, Marsha, were among the first island residents, renting a club-era employee home in 1955 and then constructing a dwelling on the ocean side. The State Supreme Court ruled in 1955 that it was legal to tax housing units on leased land. However, to encourage island development, Glynn County did not collect taxes. In 1963, the county taxation of Jekyll began after complaints were made by the board of education. (Courtesy of the Atlanta History Center.)

Following the resignation of J.D. Compton in September 1955, Governor Griffin appointed car dealer Fred Aldred (front row, center, *c.* 1956) to fill the vacant Authority position. In October 1955 the Legislative Economy Committee suggested that Jekyll be sold and Governor Griffin agreed. Another legislative committee in January 1956 investigated the island and concluded that Jekyll should remain state owned and house lots leased. These proposals were accepted and in June 1956 real estate agent James Asher (front row, left) was hired as the island manager. It was hoped that Asher could increase lot rentals. Others in the photograph include Authority board members, island employees, and members of the Pirates Club. (Courtesy of Tallu Scott.)

Rep. Robert Scoggin of Rome, Georgia, pictured *c.* 1995, chaired the 1956 legislative committee. The committee, following a review, advocated retaining Jekyll. It seemed the island was finally out of politics. However, during a July 1956 celebration, it was reported that alcohol was sold on the island. This incident, along with six negative articles about Jekyll in the *Atlanta Constitution*, prompted Governor Griffin to freeze Authority funds. Griffin proclaimed once again that either the entire or part of the island should be sold. Representative Scoggin remained vocal about the committee's conclusions and reiterated this to Griffin in a special report. Senator-elect John Drinkard, another member of the committee, summed up the situation in a July 26, 1956 *Atlanta Constitution* article by stating, "This is much to do about nothing." (Courtesy of Martha Scoggin.)

The Charcoal House Restaurant, pictured above in the 1950s, was built in a section of the White Beach House around 1956. John Crooms, the father-in-law of Jimmy Dykes, operated the eating establishment. By the late 1950s the Charcoal House was managed by Wesley and Helen Millican. The Millicans originally opened a food stand called the Big Dip Dairy Bar in 1956. The Big Dip, seen below in the 1950s, was located in the parking lot adjacent to the White Beach House and sold hot dogs, soft drinks, and ice cream. It was torn down in the 1960s. The Charcoal House Restaurant operated under the name Jekyll Sandwich Hut in the 1960s and 1970s. It was the Shoreline Restaurant in the early 1980s and Shuckers Restaurant in the mid-1980s. Currently called Blackbeard's, the restaurant was taken over by the Authority in the 1990s. (Both courtesy of the Jekyll Island Museum.)

In April 1956, the Authority awarded a contract to erect an amusement park on the island to Harvey Smith. According to the lease, land adjacent the ocean and south of the White Beach House could be developed into a theme park. Smith, the owner of the Southern Miniature Railroad Company at Calloway Gardens in Pine Mountain, Georgia, named the Jekyll attraction Peppermint Land Amusement Park. Seen above in the 1950s is the entrance booth to Peppermint Land and the parking lot. The Ferris wheel, pictured below in the late 1950s, was destroyed by Hurricane Dora in 1964. (Both courtesy of the Jekyll Island Museum.)

Peppermint Land Amusement Park, which operated for ten years, consisted of an assortment of rides, including a small roller coaster, go-carts, and a miniature train. Pictured above *c.* 1962, Brunswick residents Ken Tollison and Billy Inman stand in front of the roller coaster. Below, *c.* 1959, Billy Inman races around the go-cart track. In August 1962 baby loggerhead turtles swarmed the train tracks of the park and temporarily closed several rides. A ranger from the State Game and Fish Commission and two state patrolmen carefully gathered the turtles into boxes and safely deposited them on the beach. The turtles were attracted to the lights of the park and upon hatching traveled toward the illumination. Harvey Smith remarked in a *Brunswick News* article on August 22, 1962 that this is "a real coincidence." After checking his records, Smith noticed that baby loggerhead turtles had also swarmed the train tracks on the same date the previous year. (Both courtesy of Dr. W.O. and Ms. Beebe Inman.)

The wharf located in the then-called "Millionaires Village" was leased in May 1956 to Laurence Miller Sr. "Larry" Miller, pictured at left in a bowtie c. 1959, worked as the architect and engineer for the Authority in the mid- and late 1950s. The wharf was turned into a marina and the dock extended for additional mooring space. Other improvements included a grocery and supply store, a dock master's apartment, an electric boat hoist, and a brick restroom and shower facility. (Courtesy of Sam and Elizabeth Scarboro.)

Larry Miller, seen here in the late 1950s, named the wharf the Jekyll Island Marina. In 1959 Miller transferred the marina lease to Capt. Howard Doughty. In January 1960 Captain Doughty, mentally unstable and in financial trouble, struck his wife Catherine 25 times in the head with a bronze candlestick holder. Ms. Doughty, sleeping in the dock master's apartment when the incident occurred, died a few days after the attack. Howard Doughty apparently asked Catherine to commit suicide with him but she refused. Following the killing, Howard Doughty was nowhere to be found. About a week later, his body was discovered in Jekyll Creek approximately one mile south of the marina. Larry Miller took the lease back over soon after the tragedy. (Courtesy of Laurence Miller Jr.)

Jimmy Self was hired as the island golf pro and greens keeper in early April 1955. Since the back nine of the original club course was destroyed in construction of the perimeter road, only nine holes of golf were available for play. Self, two employees, and numerous prisoners worked throughout the summer of 1955 renovating the remaining holes. Although by September it was proclaimed the course was ready for operation, the golf links were most likely used only in a limited capacity. Self resigned in October 1955, and in April 1956, Tommy Bean was hired to take over as the golf pro. A club-era structure on the golf course, seen above in the 1950s, was utilized as the pro shop. Pictured below, c. 1956, Tommy Bean putts on the first hole of the course—dubbed the Dune Course—as greens assistant Lorenzo Walker prepares to pull the flag. (Above courtesy of the Jekyll Island Museum; below courtesy of Tommy Bean.)

Before accepting the job at Jekyll, Tommy Bean was the golf pro at Trion Golf Course near LaFayette, Georgia. A skilled player, Bean won numerous regional tournaments and, in 1956, was in the quarterfinals of the National Publinx Tournament. For several years, Tommy and Margie Bean lived with their children, Andy and Tina, in the du Bignon Cottage, a home located in the Historic District. Their son Andy has been a successful PGA golfer. Pictured in the early 1960s, Tommy Bean poses with "The Strongman" Paul Anderson, a gold medallist in the 1956 Olympics, who set 18 American and 9 World Records in weightlifting. In 1957 he was acknowledged in the *Guinness Book of World Records* for back lifting 6,270 pounds. His greatest achievement, however, was the formation of the Paul Anderson Youth Home, a safe haven for troubled young men. (Courtesy of Tommy Bean.)

A driving contest, a hole-in-one challenge, and an exhibition golf match took place at Jekyll on July 21, 1956. Pictured here c. 1956, from left to right, Hobart Manley, Tommy Bean, Mike Barber, and Pete Coleman participated in the exhibition golf match. The golfing events were coincided with festivities celebrating the removal of the Jekyll Bridge toll. Mike Barber was the golf pro at the Brunswick Golf Club. Hobart Manley and Pete Coleman, both highly talented amateur golfers, competed in numerous regional tournaments. (Courtesy of Tommy Bean.)

The driving time to Jekyll from Brunswick and St. Simons Island was drastically reduced with the July 18, 1956 opening of the Sydney Lanier Bridge over the Brunswick River. Since a fee was charged for crossing the Sydney Lanier Bridge, the toll to Jekyll was eliminated. In honor of the toll removal a daylong celebration took place on July 21, 1956. Festivities included a motorcycle race and trick riding contest sponsored by the Golden Isles Motorcycle Club, a fishing tournament and a boat race at the Jekyll Island Marina, an exhibition match at the Dunes Course, a diving demonstration and beauty contest at the Jekyll Island Hotel pool, and a fireworks display on the beach. Seen above c. 1956, spectators pose by the swimming pool of the Jekyll Island Hotel. That evening at the hotel, Nathan Jones and the Original Washboard Band and organist Evelyn Wilson entertained revelers. Nathan Jones (pictured below, on the left of the front row) and other members of the Washboard Band, including James Killens (second from right), perform for a large crowd of people. (Above courtesy of the Jekyll Island Museum; below courtesy of Ophelia Killens.)

During the toll removal celebration, a beauty contest was held at the swimming pool of the Jekyll Island Hotel. Single women between the ages of 16 and 24 were invited to compete. Pictured above c. 1956, competitors wear bathing suits in front of the Dr. Walter Belknap James memorial wall. Sixteen-year-old Kathryn Ruark from Bostwick, Georgia, pictured at left, was declared the winner and given the title "Miss Jekyll Island." Shortly after the toll removal festivities, Governor Griffin learned that beer had been sold at the White Beach House and at the Jekyll Island Hotel. Furious over the sale of alcohol, the governor declared that Jekyll should be sold and the money used to buy an atomic reactor or fund a science center at the University of Georgia. (Both courtesy of the Jekyll Island Museum.)

Four

FABULOUS JEKYLL ISLAND

"The brightest gem in Georgia's Golden Isles, Jekyll Island will be your favorite for its light-hearted way of life, its brilliant flowers and plants, and wildlife. Whatever your pleasure, you'll find it at Jekyll Island—broad white beaches, seaside and championship golf courses, camping, picnic areas, boating, fishing, fresh water lake fishing on island, tennis, or just plain loafing. All these and more are yours at fabulous Jekyll Island." This is an excerpt from an early 1960s brochure entitled "Jekyll Island, The Year-Round Family Beach Resort." The photograph was taken in the late 1950s. (Courtesy of the Jekyll Island Museum.)

In February 1957 the Georgia Legislature restructured the Jekyll Island State Park Authority and made all its members elected state officials. At the time, the members were Attorney General Eugene Cook, State Auditor B.E. Thrasher, Public Service Commissioner Matt L. McWhorter, State Parks Department director John W. Brinson Jr., and Secretary of State Ben W. Forston Jr. At the first meeting, Forston, seen here in the 1960s, was elected chair. The board's first action was a review of the lease agreements. For this task Assistant Attorney General A.J. Hartley was asked to be the legal advisor. (Courtesy of the Jekyll Island Museum.)

An automobile accident in 1929 left Ben W. Forston Jr. confined to a wheelchair. This adversity became an asset in the 1947 three-governor controversy. Since new government business could not be authorized without the state seal affixed to the order, Forston hid the seal under the cushion of his wheelchair until the governorship dilemma was resolved. Forston, seen here c. 1967 emceeing the island's Second Annual Easter Egg Hunt, was a member of the Authority until his death in May 1979. (Courtesy of the Jekyll Island Museum.)

In the late 1950s, A.J. Hartley, seen at right c. 1963 reviewing old records of the Jekyll Island Club, worked part-time as the Authority's attorney. Hartley's relationship with Jekyll started in 1947 when he administered the condemnation proceedings for the state. In 1957 state park employee John Mann was hired to replace John Asher as the island manager. In reality, however, A.J. Hartley supervised the island, as Mann could do nothing without his approval first. In September 1960 Hartley retired as assistant attorney general and began working daily on Jekyll. Hartley, given the title of executive secretary by the Authority, handled everything from hiring employees to overseeing construction projects. (Courtesy of the Jekyll Island Museum.)

Island employees and friends call A.J. Hartley "Judge" or "Judge Hartley." Although he arbitrated accident cases in 1936 and 1937 for the State Industrial Commission, the title of judge was honorary. In 1961 Hartley and his wife, Thelma, purchased a house on Beachview Drive. In the 1960s Thelma was often seen driving a Red Bug replica. The vehicle, popular during the club era, was reproduced with the thought of creating more for rental purposes. The idea was never implemented, and the Red Bug replica was donated to the Jekyll Island Museum. Pictured c. 1966 at the airport dedication, Judge Hartley displays whelk shells to elected officials. (Courtesy of the Jekyll Island Museum.)

In April 1957 the State Chamber of Commerce organized a committee of six business owners to offer suggestions about island development. Included on the committee were resort and hotel proprietor Horace Caldwell and two officials from the Sea Island Company—Alfred Jones and former Authority member Jim Compton. The group suggested that the Authority follow the Roberts & Company Master Plan as much as possible when developing Jekyll. The construction of an airport in the vicinity of the island's grass airstrip, seen above in the early 1960s, was one of the improvements called for by the master plan. (Courtesy of the Jekyll Island Museum.)

A glimpse of the location where the main convention center was eventually erected is pictured here, c. 1958. James Asher, the island manager during the restructuring of the State Park Authority, hoped to give the new board a favorable impression of Jekyll. Realizing that Ben W. Forston preferred a shoreline clean of debris, Asher had island employees rake up and remove tidal wrack from the entire beach before his first scheduled visit. Amusingly, days of work were performed in vain when on the day of Forston's arrival, tons of marsh cordgrass, usually the main component of shore wrack at Jekyll, washed up along the entire beach. In the 1950s it was not realized that sea vegetation facilitated in the creation of dunes and sandy beaches. (Courtesy of the Jekyll Island Museum.)

The first developmental undertaking by the new Authority was the construction of a paved walkway along the seashore, seen above c. 1957. During this project, the remaining sand dunes were bulldozed. The thoroughfare, called the concrete boardwalk, connected two motel sites that were approximately one and three-fourths mile apart. Ben W. Forston was confident that the improvement, a project design in the Roberts & Company Master Plan, would encourage oceanside development. Located intermittently along the boardwalk, seen below c. 1958, were benches, water fountains, and outdoor showers. Palm trees were removed from wooded areas and planted in a row parallel to the walkway. (Both courtesy of the Jekyll Island Museum.)

By autumn 1956 two areas shaded by live oaks and bordering the beach were cleared of undergrowth and developed for outdoor dining and cooking. One of the regions, named the South Picnic Area, was located south of the entrance roads between Beachview Drive and the ocean. The second picnic ground, called the North Picnic Area, was on the north end of the island adjacent Beachview Drive and the sea. In 1960 the South Picnic Area was moved one-half mile south of its original location to allow for the construction of a motel. Around 1987 the North Picnic Area, pictured above c. 1960, was closed due to erosion problems and an artificial dune system established in the location. (Courtesy of the Jekyll Island Museum.)

The Authority decided in 1958 to manufacture concrete items such as benches, tables, signposts, cooking grills, and water fountains, and a small concrete products plant was created in the former wagon and tool shed of the Jekyll Island Club. The pieces of outdoor equipment, primarily used in the picnic areas, were also placed in various locations around the island. Pictured here in the late 1950s, a small picnic area overlooks the marsh in a region adjacent Riverview Drive. (Courtesy of the Jekyll Island Museum.)

In December 1956 Clam Creek Picnic Area, seen above in the 1960s, was created at the northern tip of Jekyll. Due to erosion, fallen trees adorn the beach near the Clam Creek inlet and marsh. In the late 1950s the beach was briefly called Jekyll Roots. But in the 1960s the area became commonly referred to as Driftwood Beach. Pictured at right in the 1950s, vacationer Susan Brender poses on an overturned tree at the north end. A fourth picnic ground, St. Andrews Picnic Area, was developed in September 1960 on the southern tip of the island. (Above courtesy of South Georgia Conference of the United Methodist Church archives; right courtesy of Susan Bagwell.)

During the summer of 1957, approximately 10 lifeguard stands were placed on the beach from the South Picnic Area to the North Picnic Area, and young people were hired to work from June to August as lifeguards. Island visitors, pictured above in the 1950s, spend time on the beach as a lifeguard surveys the region from a stand. Also in the photograph, a lifeguard platform erected in the late 1940s is visible in the distance. Pictured below c. 1959, Roy Rose, a Jekyll lifeguard from 1957 to 1959, stands in front of a lifeguard station. Rose later worked as the postmaster for the Jekyll Island post office, serving in that position from January 1990 to his retirement in January 2000. Lifeguards were hired every summer at Jekyll until the mid-1980s when the practice was discontinued due to the opening of the Summer Waves Water Park. (Both courtesy of the Jekyll Island Museum.)

In late 1957 or early 1958 the Authority obtained a tram for the purpose of offering riding tours of the island. Trips around Jekyll began from Indian Mound Cottage. Adults could ride the tram, called the Mule Train, for 25¢ and children for 10¢. Pictured above, c. 1959, museum curator Tallu Fish reposes on the tram with members of her family. The tour was discontinued in the 1960s. (Courtesy of Tallu Fish Scott.)

This last known ship to transport slaves to America was the *Wanderer*, which arrived secretly at Jekyll on November 29, 1858. The cooking pot used to prepare meals for the captives was brought ashore and used to feed the 409 slaves, who were quickly sold to various plantation owners. Officials discovered the incident and prosecuted everyone involved. Repercussions were limited though, and the harshest penalty was the confiscation of the *Wanderer*. The Jekyll Island Club displayed the mess kettle for years in front of Faith Chapel. Former club gardener Wesley Wellman recalls planting flowers in it during the 1920s. From the 1950s to the 1970s, the kettle was displayed in various outdoor locations. (Courtesy of the Jekyll Island Museum.)

In the summer of 1957, work began to convert the Gould indoor tennis court—the only part of the Gould Playhouse left from the fire of 1950—into a convention hall. The project was completed by May 1958 and the first function held at the auditorium was an Elks Club meeting. The auditorium, seen above in the late 1950s, held approximately 850 people and could be rented by the hour or by the day. In the 1950s and 1960s the auditorium was often used by regional high schools for dances. According to Joe McDonough, a local concert promoter in the 1960s, singers Diana Ross and Dionne Warwick entertained on separate occasions in the hall. The band Second Coming, whose members eventually became part of the Allman Brothers band, also gave a performance here in1968 for the graduating class of Glynn Academy. Pictured below in the 1960s, the Gould Auditorium is set up for a Jaycees convention. By the 1970s this convention hall was no longer in use. (Both courtesy of the Jekyll Island Museum.)

A new golf clubhouse, seen above in the late 1950s or early 1960s, was built and in use by May 1958. Located on the nine-hole Dune Course, the structure was made with bricks from a razed cottage once owned by newspaper magnate Joseph Pulitzer. Materials for the roof came from the Authority's abandoned sawmill and the fireplace was made from ballast rocks from Quarantine Island. Quarantine Island, located on the Brunswick River, was a stopping point for all ships arriving in the port city in the 1800s. The stopover was required to keep vessels from bringing yellow fever and other diseases into the community. An 18-hole miniature golf course was also built adjacent to the golf clubhouse. Guests were charged 35¢ in 1961 to play the course, seen below in the late 1950s or early 1960s. (Both courtesy of the Jekyll Island Museum.)

Two new bathhouses, built with corrugated roofs, opened in June 1958 at opposite ends of the concrete boardwalk. Unidentified vacationers are pictured above in the early 1960s at the South Public Bath House, and the North Public Bath House is pictured below in the early 1960s. Designed by Atlanta architect Pope H. Fuller, each structure contained restrooms, showers, lockers, and a concession stand. By the summer of 1959 two concrete shelters, used as concession stands, were erected along the walkway. Due to concrete deterioration, all of the buildings were torn down in the 1980s and the bathhouses replaced with wooden, octagonal-shaped pavilions. (Both courtesy of the Jekyll Island Museum.)

The Dolphin Club lounge and restaurant, seen above c. 1959, was located in front of the Dolphin Motel. The interior included a lobby with restrooms, a kitchen, a dining room, two small private dining areas, a business office, and a nightclub. In the early years, entertainment came mainly from local dance bands and jazz ensembles. But, in 1961, blues musician B.B. King performed, and by 1964, concert promoter Charlie Cross was bringing popular blues and R&B entertainers to the Dolphin Club including Clarence Carter, Tyrone Davis, Millie Jackson, Li'l Willie Johnson, Percy Sledge, Bobby Thomas and the Afros, and Big T and the Upsetters. Pictured below in the early 1960s, the Dolphin Club and Motor Hotel, the St. Andrews Auditorium, the Beach House, and the cleared house lots of St. Andrews subdivision are visible from the air. Due to a lack of business, the Dolphin Club and Motor Hotel closed in June 1966. (Both courtesy of the Jekyll Island Museum.)

To maintain "separate but equal" facilities, a small auditorium for black citizens was erected in June 1960 near the Dolphin Club lounge and restaurant. Dubbed the St. Andrews Auditorium, the structure was maintained and operated by the Authority. Because of segregation laws in Georgia, several conventions initially scheduled on the island were canceled. For instance, in 1960 the AmVets called off a planned conference and in 1961 the International Association of Milk and Food Sanitarians changed their meeting from Jekyll to another location. Both groups cited that the cancellations were due to having members of different ethnic backgrounds unable to meet together. In the early 1960s the St. Andrews Auditorium, pictured above in the early 1960s, was primarily used for family reunions and dance events. In 1964 an Otis Redding concert took place at the auditorium. But, by the mid-1960s the building was rarely utilized. With the enactment of desegregation laws, the then-called Aquarama convention center became the meeting hub for all visitors to Jekyll. (Courtesy of the Jekyll Island Museum.)

Paving of the streets in the St. Andrews subdivision, as well as the access roads and parking area near the St. Andrews Auditorium, began in June 1960. By the late 1950s or early 1960s three lots had been leased in the residential area. As in the other subdivisions on the island, people were initially hesitant to *rent* a house site. Pictured above *c.* 1960, the road and sign leading to the St. Andrews Beach facilities are visible. (Courtesy of the Jekyll Island Museum.)

In 1958 an apartment complex was erected opposite of the Wanderer Motel. Bricks for the structure came from the razed Oglethorpe Hotel in Brunswick. Financed by James Whaley, John Minter, Myd Harris, and Carley Zell, the Seafarer Apartments opened in late 1959. Shortly thereafter, the Seafarer, seen here in the 1960s, was turned into a 21-unit motel. In 1965 and again in 1971, additions were built, bringing the number of rooms to around 71. From 1960 to 1984 Ed and Boofie Goodis managed the motel like a large family house, hosting a Thanksgiving dinner every season for guests. The Seafarer Inn and Suites was refurbished in 1999 by the IMIC Hotels Corporation. The water tower, behind the motel, was one of two erected in 1960 in the shape of a golf ball and tee. (Courtesy of the Jekyll Island Museum.)

The Corsair Motel, pictured here in the 1960s, was erected on the south end of the boardwalk in 1960. Named for yachts once owned by Jekyll Island Club members J.P. Morgan and J.P. Morgan Jr., the motel comprised 160 rooms. In the structure's center was the Nautilus restaurant, which incorporated numerous windows and featured tables with an ocean view. In 1980 the Corsair was renamed the Ladha Island Inn. Although dubbed in 1984 the Jekyll Inn and Resort, by 1986 it was called the Days Inn Jekyll. It was renovated by Budget Motel Incorporated in 1999, reducing the number of units to 124. (Courtesy of the Jekyll Island Museum.)

In November 1958 construction of a recreational center was planned adjacent to the beach. The structure was designed with three sections—an indoor swimming pool with triangular roof, 12 bowling alleys in a rectangular building, and a dance floor and skating rink inside a pentagonal structure. Pope H. Fuller, the architect of the bathhouses, the Gould Auditorium, and the first shopping center, planned the recreational center. In March 1959 the project was begun, but by 1960 the dance floor and skating rinks were changed to a ballroom and meeting space. Shortly thereafter, the bowling alleys were abandoned in favor of a convention and exhibit room. By the summer of 1961, the center, dubbed the Aquarama by Forston and Hartley, was completed. A 1960s aerial view of the Aquarama is pictured above, while below, contestants in a 1960s beauty pageant stand in front of the hyperbolic-shaped awnings of the Aquarama. (Both courtesy of the Jekyll Island Museum.)

The Aquarama's indoor swimming pool was proclaimed to adhere to the Amateur Athletic Union's size recommendations and in March 1963 the Jekyll Island Invitational Swimming and Diving Meet was started. A race is seen above c. 1963. That year a swimmer in the division for 9 to 10-year-olds marked the second best time nationally in the 50-yard freestyle, and national records were also broken in the backstroke and butterfly. The tournament was cancelled after 1966 because it was discovered the pool was smaller than Olympic size. Boilers heated the pool so vacationers, such as the ones below in the 1960s, could swim year-round. In 1964 the admission was $1. Due to structural corrosion the roof was razed in 1983 and around 1995 the pool filled in. (Above courtesy of Marvin Massey; below courtesy of the Jekyll Island Museum.)

In May 1961 construction began on an 18-hole golf course. Designed by golf architect Dick Wilson, the course was built in two phases. The first nine holes were completed by November 1962. Shortly thereafter, in January 1963, the Dune Course and the newly built nine-hole course were used for play in the Georgia State PGA golf tournament. Pictured above in the 1960s is the new nine-hole course. The last nine holes of the course were finished by early 1965. Dubbed in the 1960s the Championship Course, the greens featured a large man-made pond and were played starting from the golf clubhouse located near the ocean. Below c. 1965, prisoners lay drainpipes on fairway number 11 of the Championship Course. Prison laborers, brought over to the island from Jesup, Georgia, were used in the late 1950s and the 1960s on several Authority projects. Occasionally, prisoners escaped and hid in various areas of the island. (Above courtesy of the Jekyll Island Museum; below courtesy of Johnny Paulk.)

Professional golfer Sam Snead came to the island in May 1961 to endorse the opening of Sam Snead's Buccaneer Motor Lodge, a motel that had leased the rights to use his name for promotional purposes. During the visit, Sam Snead gave a golf clinic at the motel, signed autographs, and then participated in an exhibition match at the golf course with Tommy Bean, Hobart Manley, and Gene Dahl Bender. Mr. Snead, seen on Jekyll at right c. 1961, visited the island in 1942 as a guest of the Jekyll Island Club. Pictured below, c. early 1960s, the motel sign bearing Snead's name is discerned. (At right courtesy of Johnny Paulk; below courtesy of the Jekyll Island Museum.)

Sam Snead's Buccaneer Motor Lodge opened south of the Corsair Motel in May 1961. Motel Properties, Inc., a company then operated by James Boatwright Jr., Allen Veal, J. Milo Wammock, and L.W. Smith, built the 96-unit structure. By 1962 the use of golfer Sam Snead's name was discontinued and the motel became the Buccaneer Motor Lodge. The entrance to the motel is pictured above in the 1960s. In 1967 and 1969 additions were made to the motel, increasing the number of rooms to 206. It became the Quality Inn Buccaneer in 1985; by the 1990s it was named the Clarion Resort Buccaneer. (Courtesy of the Jekyll Island Museum.)

In 1960 construction began on a Holiday Inn south of the Buccaneer Motor Lodge. Opening by June 1961, the motel had 106 rooms and a swimming pool in the shape of the state of Georgia. In January 1963 State Rep. William "Bill" Stuckey, vice president of Stuckey's Inc., purchased the Holiday Inn and renamed it Stuckey's Carriage Inn. Stuckey's Inc. at the time owned 11 candy and pecan stores and was reputedly the largest manufacturer of pecan candies in the world. Stuckey's Carriage Inn is observed above in the 1960s. By the early 1970s the motel was called the Atlantic Carriage Inn and in 1980 the Ramada Inn. Around 1998 it was remodeled. (Courtesy of the Jekyll Island Museum.)

Off-duty law enforcement officers from Brunswick were hired in the 1950s to patrol Jekyll, and the commissary building in the Historic District became the police headquarters. In 1957 the island speed limit became 35 miles per hour, with 25 miles per hour on the east-west roads. In May 1960 Gov. Ernest Vandiver established a State Patrol Post on the island and assigned it four state troopers. Trooper Embree, seen above in the 1960s, was one of the first state patrol officers serving the Jekyll community. The State Patrol Post has been in several locations including Villa Marianna and Crane Cottage. In 1985 it was placed in the former causeway gas station. (Courtesy of the Jekyll Island Museum.)

In 1962 a fire department was established at the motor pool—a garage building constructed in late 1961 on Stable Road. The Authority purchased an ambulance and several firefighting vehicles and hired five firefighters to operate the equipment. Fire Chief Jesse Owens (standing far right) and four other firefighters are pictured above c. 1962 at the motor pool. In 1958 ten three-bedroom homes were constructed near the campground for Authority workers; by the 1960s many of the firefighters were residing in these houses. A fire station was built on Stable Road near the motor pool in the late 1960s. (Courtesy of the Jekyll Island Museum.)

A second shopping center, developed by Wright Parker and Cecil Mason, was erected adjacent the Authority-built shopping center. By June 1964, Whittle's gift shop, Altman's dress store, O'Quinn's clothier for men, Kentucky Fried Chicken, Albert Crew's Seafood House, Seven-Eleven food store, Georgia Burger House, Parker Realty Company, a coin laundry, and Quinton Williams barber and beauty shop were in operation. The second shopping center is seen above in the late 1960s. Storeowners rented space from Parker and Mason, who leased the land from the Authority. The shopping center, pictured below in the 1960s, featured a butterfly awning. In 1995 the shopping center was renovated. (Both courtesy of the Jekyll Island Museum.)

Earl Hill, a former club caddy, started a golf tournament on the island in 1964. He is pictured on the far right with his brothers Arthur and Ray in the late 1960s. To help manage the golf competition—called the Southeastern Golf Tournament—Earl Hill formed a social organization called the Frontier Club. They found financial sponsors, created a souvenir program, and organized the tournament. The tournament, sometimes nicknamed "The Classic" by Hill, attracted numerous golf professionals to the island, including Lee Elder, Jim Dent, Zeke Hartfield, George Johnson, Ted Rhodes, Charlie Stifford, Nate Starks, and Jim Thorpe. Lee Elder won the tournament in 1966 and 1967. Jimmy Devoe, proprietor of the first golf school owned by a black American, was a regular tournament participant. Earl Hill co-owned the Blue Inn nightclub on St. Simons Island, operated a taxi service, and worked for the Wanderer Motel. (Courtesy of Dr. Ray Hill.)

In 1964 Earl Hill and the Frontier Club held an Otis Redding concert at the St. Andrews Auditorium to raise money for the first tournament. That year at the awards ceremony Jerry Butler performed at the Aquarama, officially desegregating the convention center. Other award ceremonies boasted entertainers such as Wilson Pickett, Joe Simon, and Percy Sledge. In 1975, at the eleventh tournament, 71 golf professionals vied for the first-place prize of $2,500. Pictured above in the 1970s, Earl Hill (second from right) poses with Hall of Fame football player Jim Brown (far right), Glynn Academy associate principal Clyde Williams (second from left), and an unidentified person. Hill hosted the final Southeastern Golf Tournament in the early 1980s. (Courtesy of Sandra Mungin.)

In 1963 Genoa and Mamie Martin erected the first home in St. Andrews subdivision, seen above c. 1972. In the 1930s Mr. Martin (seen at left in the 1970s) worked briefly for the Jekyll Island Club. But from 1948 to 1985 he was the assistant director, then later director, of Selden Park in Brunswick. Martin was instrumental in bringing jazz greats Duke Ellington and Cab Calloway and entertainers James Brown and The Drifters to Brunswick. He hosted a radio program every Sunday on WGIG. Mamie Martin was a nurse at the Brunswick Hospital and a plaque was placed there in the 1980s honoring her for service to the community. (Both courtesy of Sandra Mungin.)

Joseph Henry and Lillian Armstrong, seen at right in the 1970s, constructed the second house in the St. Andrews subdivision in 1964. In 1928 Mr. Armstrong worked for the Jekyll Island Club as the Indian Mound Cottage caretaker. Mrs. Armstrong, in the 1920s and 1930s, often came to Jekyll to visit relatives employed by the club. The couple's fondness for the area prompted them to move to the island in later years. Mr. Armstrong, retiring in 1973, spent 45 years with the United States Postal Service. Lillian Armstrong, a self-employed beautician, worked during WW II as a private duty nurse and made special deliveries for the post office. The Armstrong's home is pictured below in the late 1960s or early 1970s. In 1965 Dr. J. Clinton and Mrs. Josephine Wilkes built the third house on the south end of the island on Beachview Drive, slightly past St. Andrews subdivision. The other homes in the St. Andrews residential area would not be erected until after 1971. (Right courtesy of Joseph Henry and Lillian Armstrong; below courtesy of Sandra Mungin.)

An indoor tennis court, built by the club in 1929, was refurbished and made available free of charge to players in the early 1960s. Five outdoor courts were also constructed, and by 1965, a brick clubhouse was erected. It was called the Golden Isles Tennis Club in the 1960s; by the early 1970s it was renamed the J.P. Morgan Tennis Center. In 1975 three more courts and a practice wall were added. The first tennis professional, Gordon Davis, was hired in 1972; from 1974 to 1988 Bill Mitchell worked as the tennis professional. The indoor court and the tennis clubhouse are pictured above in the 1970s; tennis players in the 1970s are seen below on the outdoor courts. In 1988 Pete Poole was hired to manage a new tennis center with 13 courts near the main golf clubhouse. (Both courtesy of the Jekyll Island Museum.)

Erosion problems were caused by the removal of sand dunes, and in 1964, trucks, bulldozers, and draglines were used to erect a granite rock bulwark along areas of the beach. In September 1964 Hurricane Dora, pounding the island with strong winds, heavy rains, and large waves, prompted the Office of Emergency Planning to allot funds for the increasing of the revetment wall. Erosion caused by the Hurricane is observed above c. 1964. At right, Diane Colvin and several off-duty sailors from Mayport, Florida, sunbathe in front of the bulwark in the 1960s. The granite rock revetment project was further expanded in 1975. (Above courtesy of the Jekyll Island Museum; right courtesy of Diane Wilkes.)

On January 15, 1915, AT&T president and club member Theodore N. Vail participated from the island in the opening of the first telephone line across the United States. In 1965 a telephone display was placed near Indian Mound Cottage and a celebration honoring the event's 50th anniversary took place on January 22. The Georgia Chapter of the Telephone Pioneers of America, an organization established by Vail in 1911, financed the display. (Courtesy of the South Georgia Conference of the United Methodist Church archives.)

Retired telephone worker Herman Murdock (fourth from right) and retired telephone operator Clara Horton (far right) were invited to the 50th anniversary celebration. In 1915 Murdock repaired the telephone line shortly before the call, enabling Jekyll to participate, and Horton managed the Clubhouse switchboard. Dr. Sidney Vail, a St. Simons Island dentist and relative of Theodore Vail, is second from right. From the dedication, the group moved to Stuckey's Carriage Inn for a luncheon and telephone call re-enactment. Using a switchboard found in the attic of Crane Cottage, Ben W. Forston Jr. (third from right) telephoned Theodore Vail's great grandniece Margaret Vail Foster in San Jose, California. The event concluded with Telephone Pioneer vice president Larry P. Morgan (second from left) telephoning AT&T president H.M. Romnes in New York. W.B. Adams, the designer of the telephone display, is standing on the far left. (Courtesy of the *Brunswick News*.)

While inspecting property lines in April 1965, Authority employees found two gun emplacements on the south end of Jekyll. U.S. Department of Interior officials and historians from Fort Frederica were asked to inspect the site and date the gun carriages. The answer, however, came from St. Simons Island resident Catherine Clark. She recalled that her father, James Clark—a club boat captain—told her that gun batteries were placed on the island during the Spanish-American War. One of the emplacements is above, c. 1965. Due to accretion, the emplacements no longer overlook the ocean. (Courtesy of the Jekyll Island Museum.)

In 1966 Dr. Charles Fairbanks, a University of Florida archaeologist, examined the Horton House and surrounding tabby ruins to find evidence of the original floors, porches, and roofs. Above c. 1966, two students investigate remnants of a tabby structure. Judge Hartley stated in a July 10, 1966 *Atlanta Journal-Constitution* article that the Authority planned to restore the Horton House as well as the cottages in the "Millionaires Village." Restoration architect J. Everette Fauber Jr., landscape architect Clermont H. Lee, and interior architect Marguerite Valk were hired to prepare plans for the restoration. From 1966 to 1969 the team interviewed former club employees and obtained various historical documents. Due to Authority funds going to other projects, their plans were never utilized. (Courtesy of the Jekyll Island Museum.)

In the late 1950s and early 1960s several Christian denominations shared Faith Chapel, built during the club era. However, in 1962, construction of a Presbyterian church was started on a site near the Jekyll airstrip. By April 1963, Rev. David Boozer was holding services there. The Jekyll Presbyterian Community Church, pictured above in the late 1960s, was designed to hold a large number of vacationers as well as sustain the needs of the island residents. In the late 1960s and early 1970s, well-known author Dr. Charlie W. Shedd conducted the worship services at the church. (Courtesy of the Jekyll Island Museum.)

A Methodist church was planned in September 1962, but the actual construction did not start until 1965. Seen above at the September 5, 1965 groundbreaking ceremony, Methodist dignitaries and island residents watch as Jekyll homeowner Millard Dusenbury shovels the site of the church. Serving as the pastor from 1962 to 1966, Rev. James Panell (fourth from left) was the first Methodist minister. The Episcopal Church of St. Richard and the St. Francis Xavier Roman Catholic Church also utilize the Jekyll Island United Methodist Church for services. (Courtesy of the South Georgia Conference of the United Methodist Church archives.)

Through funding obtained in 1965 from the Federal Aviation Agency, the Georgia Department of Industry and Trade, and the Jekyll Island Authority, the grass airstrip was paved and a small airport building constructed. Although the runway was extended in 1967, the 3,715-foot landing strip is only usable by small planes. In the late 1960s the Authority hosted a series of Fly-In conventions, where planes of a certain model were invited to vacation on the island. At the conventions, plane owners were encouraged to participate in arranged activities that included sightseeing, parties, and historical presentations by museum curator Tallu Fish. The runway is seen above in the 1960s. Pictured below, c. 1966, is the airport building with a control tower on the roof. The control tower was removed after the Fly-In conventions were discontinued in the early 1970s. (Both courtesy of the Jekyll Island Museum.)

Throughout the 1960s the number of conventions held on the island escalated. While in 1962 there were 126 conventions, by 1965 the total had risen to 430. During this period the Church of God Festival, seen above in the 1960s, was the largest convention. It coincided with the Old Testament Festival of Tabernacles and attracted thousands of followers. Meeting at Jekyll for the first time in 1962, the convention boasted over 8,000 people by 1970. The last Church of God festival of this size occurred on the island in 1977. (Courtesy of the Jekyll Island Museum.)

Children and parents participate in the second annual Easter Egg Hunt. In May 1966 a hunt for 10,000 colored eggs was started on the island. Co-sponsored by the Georgia Egg Commission, the Pure Oil Company, Stuckey's Inc., and the Jekyll Island Authority, the event drew an estimated crowd of 8,000 to 10,000 people. A hidden golden egg, located by deciphering a series of clues, won the finder in 1966 a $100 savings bond and a trip to Stuckey's candy manufacturing plant. In 1967 the award was $1,000. (Courtesy of the Jekyll Island Museum)

Debris and broken pieces of the sign that once adorned the entrance to Peppermint Land Amusement Park are viewed above, c. 1965. Harvey Smith, proprietor of Peppermint Land, stated in July 1965 that he was closing the park. Earlier that year his lease was raised from three to fifteen percent net profit and switched to a month-by-month basis. Smith said he could not operate without the security of a longer lease. (Courtesy of the Jekyll Island Museum.)

When the Dolphin Club and Motor Hotel closed in June 1966, the structure was turned into a group camp and youth center. In the late 1960s and 1970s numerous schools, church groups, and organizations used the facilities, seen above in the early 1970s. Around 1969 athletic fields were built near the area. In June 1983, 4-H organizations, managed by the Cooperative Extension System of the University of Georgia's College of Agricultural and Environmental Sciences, took over operation of the center. A summer camp offered environmental courses to youth groups and schools. Called the Environmental Education Program, the camp became a year-round enterprise in 1987 (Courtesy of the Jekyll Island Museum.)

It was announced in 1965 that a second 18-hole golf course and larger clubhouse would be built on Captain Wylly Road. The facilities were completed in 1967 and a ceremony opening the course and clubhouse was held on December 9th. Pictured above c. 1967, Judge Hartley, Lt. Gov. George Smith, and members of the Georgia Legislature participate in the dedication of the new Pine Lakes golf course. Following the ceremony, Gov. Lester Maddox dedicated the new clubhouse, seen below in the late 1960s. It had an entrance facing the Pine Lakes course and another entrance facing the then-called Championship Course. The smaller clubhouse near the ocean remained the start of the nine-hole course. The new clubhouse and course were the last projects on the island completed under the leadership of Judge Hartley. He retired on September 30, 1967, at the age of 65. (Both courtesy of the Jekyll Island Museum.)

Five

MOST GOLDEN OF THE GOLDEN ISLES

"In the 70s my wife and I were motoring from Hobe Sound, Florida to Sea Island, Georgia and we thought a stop off on the way at Jekyll Island would be a pleasant interlude. We were amazed at the splendid way the State of Georgia had developed the property. A causeway had been built to the island; the island had evidently been zoned which was an excellent idea. The golf course and beaches were in beautiful shape. The old club house was still there and to my surprise I saw a flock of about twenty-five wild turkeys walking around near the old chapel. There was not a wild turkey on the island when the club owned it. The State of Georgia should be congratulated on the way they developed Jekyll Island," club member Dudley H. Mills writes in a 1983 letter. (Photograph *c.* late 1960s, courtesy of the Jekyll Island Museum.)

In March 1968, golf pro Johnny Paulk III took over operation of the Jekyll Island Golf Club. Seated at left in this 1960s photo, he worked from 1960 to 1968 as the assistant golf pro at the East Lake Country Club in Atlanta. Johnny and his wife, Virginia, have been congenial island hosts to countless golfers and non-golfers alike. Highly charismatic, Paulk was described in a 1966 letter written by Masters Tournament founder Bobby Jones Jr. as "a very personable young man of attractive personality. He impresses me as being very serious about his activities in the golf profession." In 1985, Gov. Joe Frank Harris named Paulk an honorary member of his staff; in 1979 Paulk was asked to be the 9th-hole announcer at the Masters Tournament, an annual distinction that in 1998 was switched to the 18th fairway. (Courtesy of Johnny Paulk.)

Indian Mound golf course, named for the Native American artifacts discovered in the vicinity of the 14th fairway, was dedicated and opened for play on May 10, 1975. The roof tiles of the restroom facilities on the 6th and 13th holes came from the Jekyll Island Club laundry, a building dismantled in the Historic District around 1974. During the golf course dedication, the Championship Course was renamed Oleander. Pictured at left, c. 1975, Johnny Paulk (second from left) poses with retired island director Horace Caldwell (second from right); Authority chair Ben Wiggins (far right); and Harvey Manley on the new 18-hole golf course. Horace Caldwell, a former director of the Georgia State Parks Department as well as a past Authority board member, replaced the retiring Judge Hartley as administrator of the island in 1967. (Courtesy of Johnny Paulk.)

In 1969 island resident and retired DuPont engineer Roger Beedle renovated Faith Chapel and Indian Mound Cottage. Authority chair Ben W. Forston Jr., island director Horace Caldwell, and other dignitaries are seen above, c. 1970, at a ceremony re-dedicating Faith Chapel. Throughout the 1970s Roger Beedle and Ken DeBellis refurbished several structures in the Historic District; in July 1977, an eleven-day ceremony—dubbed the Grand Opening of the Jekyll Club Village—took place. Visitors were invited to attend history presentations and explore several of the cottages, including Moss, Indian Mound, and Crane. In 1978 the U.S. Department of Interior designated the club structures a National Historic Landmark. (Courtesy of the Jekyll Island Museum.)

During a ceremony in January 1970, Ben Forston Jr. (center) and Horace Caldwell (right) bestowed Tallu Fish with the title "Curator Emeritus of the Jekyll Island Museum, Archivist and Historian for Jekyll Island." In a letter to Horace Caldwell dated December 31, 1969, Fish declared, "My era is gone—the old Rockefeller Museum was like one of my grand children, but I believe you should have your own set-up for the new regime. Yet, I love Jekyll too well not to be an integral part in its progress and welfare and public relations." Using a room on the first floor of the Clubhouse, Fish compiled and officially formed the museum archives in early 1970. She died August 26, 1971. (Courtesy of the Jekyll Island Museum.)

In 1967 construction began on a marina south of the island bridge. The new marina, it was proclaimed, would include fresh- and salt-water boat slips, supply stores, and restaurants. A drawing of the proposed marina is above. Using a dredge, workers created a large pond for fresh-water boat storage and a boat basin with two entrances to Jekyll Creek. A small dock was erected in the basin connected to the intra-coastal waterway. Although Capt. Beau Sam McGowan operated a charter boat briefly from the vicinity, silt deposits from the changing tides soon made the intra-coastal basin unusable. The idea of a marina designed in this manner was abandoned by the mid-1970s. From 1984 to 1996 the Ski Rixen, a cable water skiing business, operated on the dredged pond and in 1987 Summer Waves Waterpark was built between the two artificial basins. (Courtesy of the Jekyll Island Museum.)

A fishing pier was built in 1969 on the north end of the island; an aerial view of the structure is seen above. For a brief time adults were charged 50¢ and children 25¢ to fish from the pier. Although significantly used by locals and visitors alike, the fee was discontinued due to lack of profits to the lessee of the pier. (Courtesy of the Jekyll Island Museum.)

The Authority purchased a large slide in 1969 and erected the amusement in the parking lot of the Jekyll Sandwich Hut restaurant. Referred to as the Superslide, it operated on weekends and holidays and cost 15¢ a slide. Since the Superslide caused passengers to slide down too quickly when wet, it could not be used unless it was dry. Over time ocean spray salted down the slide making it practically impossible to ride. In September 1971 the amusement was dismantled and sold. (Courtesy of the Jekyll Island Museum.)

A plan was made in August 1970 to build an aquarium on six acres of land adjacent to the South Picnic Area, and it was approved by island director Horace Caldwell. Several Brunswick residents formed a company called Sea Circus, Inc. and petitioned citizens of Georgia to obtain stock in the business. An advertisement to purchase stock is seen at right, c. 1971. The aquarium, protested by many of the island residents and vacationers, was to be modeled after Marineland of Florida. The Sea Circus, according to a June 4, 1971 article in *Jekyll's Golden Islander*, would consist of "trained porpoises, sea lions, and penguins" as well as other marine animals. Although a groundbreaking ceremony took place in June of 1971, the idea did not obtain widespread approval or sufficient financial backing. By 1972 the idea of a Sea Circus aquarium was abandoned. (Courtesy of *Jekyll's Golden Islander*.)

This announcement is neither an offer to sell nor a solicitation of an offer to buy these securities. The offer is made only by the revised Prospectus and solely to bona fide residents of the State of Georgia.

NEW ISSUE   MARCH 23, 1971

SEA CIRCUS, INC.
100,000 SHARES
COMMON STOCK
PRICE $7.50 per share (Par Value 10¢)

SEA CIRCUS, INC. (the "company"), was originally incorporated under the name of Marineland of Georgia, Inc. It was organized August 20, 1970, under the laws of the State of Georgia. On September 29, 1970, the name of the corporation was changed from Marineland of Georgia, Inc., to Sea World, Inc. On March 9, 1971 the corporate name was changed to Sea Circus, Inc. The purpose of the incorporation was the operation of a marine life-type exhibit as well as the buying and selling of motels, hotels, restaurants and gift shops. The Company's principal office and place of business is located at P.O. Box 27, Jekyll Island, Georgia.

Copies of the Prospectus may be obtained from the office of the Company by mailing the coupon below:

Please send a copy of your revised Prospectus to:

Name_____

SEA WORLD, INC.   Address_____
P.O. Box 27
Jekyll Island, Ga.   City & State_____ zip_____
· 31520
I am a bona fide resident of the State of Georgia

Signed_____

119

An amphitheatre was built on Jekyll in 1972. From 1973 to 1975, performances of the musical *Drumbeats in Georgia* took place here. The musical, a scene from which is pictured below, told the story of the founding of the Georgia colony. The script was written by Paul Green, author of the North Carolina play *Unto These Hills*. In the spring of 1973 the servants' quarters and Villa Ospo Cottage, both club-era structures, were renovated and used as housing for the performers and staff members. A repertoire company from Florida State University replaced *Drumbeats in Georgia* in 1976. While the repertoire company consisted mainly of college students, professional actors were hired for the lead roles. A series of three or four musicals were presented by Florida State every summer until about 1983. From around 1983 to 1988 the University of Georgia's Department of Theatre offered summer performances at the amphitheatre. Valdosta State University, dubbed in 1993 the official State Musical Theatre of Georgia, began staging musicals here in 1989. (Both courtesy of the Jekyll Island Museum.)

Debates over selling alcohol on state-owned property began as early as the 1950s. But, the issue was not resolved on Jekyll until 1971. Through a petition created by island residents, the Authority called for a referendum to determine if alcoholic beverages could be sold. On May 18, 1971, a vote took place at Gould Auditorium with assistant island director Fred Griffith acting as election superintendent. Of the 521 registered voters on Jekyll, 223 voted in favor of the measure and 96 opposed. Island residents Nadine Rush (seated left) and her husband Ashton Rush (standing to her right) are seen in the 1970s at the Mariner's Cove, a lounge in the Wanderer Motel that received a liquor license after the vote. (Courtesy of Nadine Rush.)

A 2,200-seat auditorium, an exhibit hall, and several meeting rooms were built onto the Aquarama Convention Center and in operation by early 1975. The new facilities included eight murals by island resident Esther Stewart depicting scenes of Georgia's history. The new auditorium was dubbed the Hartley Auditorium in tribute to former island director Judge A.J. Hartley, who died in 1973; the exhibit hall in 1981 was renamed the Caldwell Exhibit Hall in honor of Horace Caldwell, island director from 1967 to 1972. The convention center was completely remodeled in 1995 and early 1996. (Courtesy of the Jekyll Island Museum.)

Larry Morris, a former Georgia state representative and past NFL football player, constructed the Sand Dollar Motel in 1971. Pictured above in the 1970s, it included 263 rooms and small apartments, a restaurant, and a lounge. Seen at left in the 1970s, Georgia Gov. Jimmy Carter, Rosalyn Carter, and their daughter Amy pose in front of the Sand Dollar Motel sign. Mr. Carter, the 39th President of the United States, vacationed at Jekyll on several occasions. and on one trip taught a class of students at the Jekyll Island Youth Center. The motel operated from 1979 to 1987 under the name Jekyll Hilton Inn. From 1992 to 1997 it was called the Best Western Jekyll Inn; since 1987 it has been called the Jekyll Inn. (Above courtesy of the Jekyll Island Museum; below courtesy of Bill Minter.)

In 1973 Howard Atherton, Arthur Crowe Jr., J.H. Henderson Jr., and David Rambo built the By The Sea hotel on the northern end of the island. Opening in March 1974, the structure included 176 one-, two-, and three-bedroom units. In May 1975 the hotel was renamed the Sheraton By The Sea. In 1981 it was dubbed the Villas By The Sea, and in 1986, a conference center was built. In 1989 the units were turned into condominiums and sold to individual buyers. The villa owners determine what company manages the leasing of units. (Courtesy of the Jekyll Island Authority.)

Penmoco, a company owned by Myd Harris, Tom Pierce, and Carley Zell, built a Holiday Inn south of the Atlantic Carriage Inn in 1972. The sand dunes and live oak trees were retained as much as possible; Sea Island Landscape architect T. Miesse Baumgardner was contracted to direct the hotel landscaping. The Holiday Inn Beach Resort, which opened in 1975, includes 205 rooms, a restaurant, and a lounge. In 1976 Servico Inc. bought the hotel. The Holiday Inn sign and entranceway appear here in the 1980s. (Courtesy of the Jekyll Island Authority.)

Like the other Christian denominations on the island, the Baptist congregation initially held services in the 1960s and early 1970s at Faith Chapel. However, in 1973, construction began on a Baptist church along Riverview Drive. By 1974 the structure was completed and available for worship. The Jekyll Island Baptist Church is pictured above c. 1974. (Courtesy of Beth Peek.)

Nancy Albright Hurd, the daughter of former club members John J. and Susan Albright, began spending winters on Jekyll with her husband, Lawrence Hurd, in 1976. During their sojourns, Ms. Hurd assisted the Jekyll Island Museum with research. In 1979, with the resignation of museum employees Ken and Tania Debellis, Nancy Hurd reluctantly took over as the museum curator. She remained the curator on a part-time basis until at least 1983; she is seen here at an island social function with her grandson Philip Schluter. In 1981 the Brunswick Library recorded an interview with Hurd where she recollected memories of growing up on Jekyll in the early 1900s. (Courtesy of Rev. Nancy Hurd Schluter.)

In 1975 Mary's Doll House, later renamed Mary Miller's Doll Museum, opened at Villa Ospo Cottage. Pictured above (right) in the 1970s is one of the display shelves in Villa Ospo. Miller, left, started the first travel agency in Brunswick in 1946 and to entice patrons to travel, she displayed dolls she obtained while vacationing at her agency. In the 1970s she exhibited her collection, which included a doll given in the early 1900s to Katherine Clark by club member Charles Stewart Maurice's son. In 1984 Mary Miller's Doll Museum moved to Brunswick (Left courtesy of Mary Miller's Doll Museum; right courtesy of the Jekyll Island Museum.)

Island resident Glenn Stauffer leased the club's power plant building and opened the Antique Automobile Museum in 1976. An avid car collector and restorer, Stauffer exhibited motor vehicles of the 1930s such as Roadsters, Phaetons, and Cadillacs. The car museum is seen above in the 1970s. Due to health reasons, Stauffer in 1983 closed the museum. The Santa's Christmas Shoppe gift store operated there from 1984 to 2001. (Courtesy of the Jekyll Island Museum.)

Prompted by a reunion with former musicians and friends from the University of Mississippi, island resident Jodie Smith formed the Jekyll Island Big Band in March 1979. Smith located musicians for the ensemble, seen above in the 1980s, by advertising in the *Brunswick News*. Sponsored initially by the Authority, the band first performed on June 9, 1979, and a 1980 album was produced by the group entitled *Georgia on My Mind*. The Big Band, while playing music of the 1930s and 1940s, also performs Latin, waltz, and contemporary songs. In 1994 resident Dr. Hal Crowe took over as the conductor. (Courtesy of Dr. Hal Crowe.)

Accomplished artists Florence and Rosario Russell Fiore retired to Jekyll in 1967. Mr. Fiore, from designing presidential gifts for foreign dignitaries to the creation of museum sculptures, sculpted his entire life. Seen at left in the 1980s in his art studio/garage, "Russ" Fiore redesigned a lapel pin originally given to WW I veterans. This eagle pin, known as the "Ruptured Duck Button," was presented to honorably discharged WW II veterans. Although given no credit, Fiore did a significant portion of the "Waving Girl" statue in Savannah, Georgia. In 1989 Florence and Russ donated artwork they produced while living on the island to the Fiore Sculpture and Art Center. Since the early 1990s, the center, formed by the Jekyll Island Museum Associates, has displayed the Fiore sculptures on the second floor of Mistletoe Cottage. Suffering from Parkinson's disease and no longer able to sculpt, Russ Fiore committed suicide in 1994. (Courtesy of *Jekyll's Golden Islander*.)

BIBLIOGRAPHY

Archive Files of the Jekyll Island Museum. Jekyll Island, Georgia.

Farrisee, A. *The Three Governor Controversy*. [On-line].www.sos.state.ga.us/capitolguide/appendixc.htm

Jekyll's Golden Islander, 1971–1985. Jekyll Island Museum Archives; *Jekyll's Golden Islander* office, Brunswick, GA.

Jekyll Island Authority Meeting Minutes, 1950–1965. Jekyll Island Museum Archives. Jekyll Island, GA.

Jekyll Island Files. Gilbert, Harrell, Gilbert, Sumerford, & Martin Law Office. Brunswick, GA.

Kimsey, T. and Kinard S. *Memories from the Marshes of Glynn: World War II*. Decatur, GA: Looking Glass Books, 1999.

Martin, H. *This Happy Isle: The Story of Sea Island and the Cloister*. Sea Island Company, 1978.

McCash,W. and McCash J. *The Jekyll Island Club: Southern Haven for America's Millionaires*. Athens, GA: The University of Georgia Press, 1989.

Schoettle, T. *A Guide to a Georgia Barrier Island: Featuring Jekyll Island with St. Simons and Sapelo Islands*. St. Simons Island, GA: Watermarks Publishing, 1996.

Tallu Fish Scrapbooks, 1954–1970. Jekyll Island Museum Archives. Jekyll Island, GA

The Brunswick News, 1946–1954. Brunswick-Glynn County Library, Brunswick, GA.

Whitaker Documents, 1949–1951. Author's Collection.

Interviews 1999–2001: Doug Adamson, Sam Altman, Joseph Henry Armstrong, Gerald Atkinson, Susan Bagwell, Mary Whitaker Bailey, Carl Baumgardner, Tommy Bean, Harry Beckel, Curtis Bell, Pat Bentley, Phillip Bluestein, Ed Brophy, Bill Brown, Bob Brown, Anne Buchan, W.W. Buckingham, Ralph Bufkin, Larry Burel, Leonard Cahoon, Jeanyne Carmouche, Betty Chandler, Kathryn Dykes Cheshire, Bob Cody, Pete Coleman, Charles Corn, Ruby Crawford, Ruth Crawford, Charlie Cross, Dr. Hal Crowe, Cannon Davidson, Gordon Davis, Jim Davis, Ken DeBellis, Lloyd Douglas, Judy Horton Duke, Jimmy Dunn, John Dykes, Lee Elder, Ann Corn Felton, Ed Garrett, Joe Gaudiello, Cliff Gawron, Edwina Gill, Steve Godley, Ed Goodis, Jim Goodis, Charles Gowen, Lorraine Gravin, Fred Griffith, Thelma Hartley, Dr. Ray Hill, Ralph Hoffmeyer, Rev. Julius C. Hope, Frog Horton, Julia Horton, Mal Hoyt, Beebe Inman, Dr. W.O. Inman, Judge Isaac Jenrette, Ophelia Killens, Morell Knight, Clermont H. Lee, Joe McDonough, Beau Sam McGowan, Jack Mckinney, Peggy McMath, Walter McNeely, Scotty McPhee, Gov. Lester Maddox, Alfred Martin, Dot Mason, Joe Mason, Marvin Massey, Gertrude Maxwell, Laurence Miller Jr., Wesley Millican, Bill Minter, Yank Moore, Sandra Mungin, Lyneath Musgrove, Beverly Myers, Bill Newberry, Mary Newberry, Ann North, Myrtle Oxford, O.V. Ottwell, Linda Dykes Pageant, Wallace Pageant, Johnny Paulk, Caesar Pavia, Beth Peek, Marshall Peek, Kenneth Picha, Vivien Picha, Eddie Pickett, Louise Pippen, Len Polezak, Murray Poole, Pete Poole, Alfonza Ramsey, Louise Ringel, Roy Rose, Nadine Rush, Elizabeth Scarboro, Sam Scarboro, Lillian Schaitberger, Judge Robert Scoggin, Tallu Fish Scott, Hoke Gilbert Smith, Linda Smith, Sam Snead, Joe Spaulding, Donna Stewart, Carmen Stovall, Linda Talmadge, Lucy Thompson, Mildred Tichnell, Dena Torkildson, F.H. Torkildson, Gov. Ernest Vandiver, Leonardo Velazquez, Sami Walker, Mike Wamock, Wesley Wellman, Don West, Bob Whitaker, Peg Whitaker, Diane Wilkes, Clyde Williams, B. J. Wilson, Jackie Yeomans, and Harold Zell.

ACKNOWLEDGMENTS

This book could not have materialized without the emotional and financial assistance of my parents, Charles and Susan Bagwell—thank you! I am indebted to Jekyll Island Museum founder Tallu Fish, whose scrapbooks greatly contributed to this project. Acknowledgments go to Lillian Schaitberger, Bob and Peg Whitaker, and Mary Whitaker Bailey for helping to set this book in motion. Sincere appreciation goes to the staff of the Jekyll Island Museum, including Warren Murphey, John Hunter, Georgia Eden, Cricket Bagley, and former employees Leslie Hicks, Karen McInnis, and Brannen Sanders. Gratitude goes to Johnny Paulk and Roy Rose for the countless times spent answering questions and identifying photographs. Recognition extends to Rick Germano, Carmen Spatola, and David Zachry for the wonderful conversations held.

I am especially thankful for the assistance and contributions from the following persons, organizations, and companies: Doug Adamson; Sam Altman; Joseph Henry Armstrong; Gerald Atkinson; Mary Whitaker Bailey; Carl Baumgardner; Tommy Bean; Harry Beckel; Curtis Bell; Pat Bentley; Phillip Bluestein; Ed Brophy; Bill Brown;, Bob Brown; Christy Brown; Cindy McDonald and Ed Schroeder of the Jekyll Island Authority; Catherine Bryan;, Anne Buchan;, W.W. Buckingham; Ralph Bufkin; Larry Burel; Leonard Cahoon; Calloway Gardens; Jim Cameron and Cary Knapp of the Brunswick-Glynn County Library;, Jeanyne Carmouche; Betty Chandler;, Kathryn Dykes Cheshire; Bob Cody; Pete Coleman; Charles Corn; Ruby Crawford; Ruth Crawford; Charlie Cross; Dr. Hal Crowe; Cannon Davidson; Gordon Davis;, Jim Davis; Ken DeBellis; Lloyd Douglas; Judy Horton Duke, Jimmy Dunn; John Dykes; Lee Elder, Greg Eow and the DeKalb Historical Society; Ann Corn Felton; *Florida Times-Union*; Troy Fore; John Eaton and Noel Watson of *Jekyll's Golden Islander*; Matt Fry and the *Brunswick News*; Ed Garrett; Joe Gaudiello; Cliff Gawron; Jim Gilbert and the Gilbert, Harrell, Gilbert, Sumerford, & Martin Law Office; Edwina Gill and the Mary Miller's Doll Museum; Sheila Godley; Steve Godley; Ed Goodis; Jim Goodis; Charles Gowen; Lorraine Gravin; Fred Griffith; Robert Haase and Glynn Camera; Thelma Hartley; Jennifer Harvey; Dr. Ray Hill; Ralph Hoffmeyer; Benjie Hodges; Rev. Julius C. Hope; Frog Horton; Julia Horton; Matt Howell; Mal Hoyt; Beebe Inman; Dr. W.O. Inman; Judge Isaac Jenrette; the JWT; Ophelia Killens; Bill King; Morell Knight; Fern Lavinder and Mary Vice of the United Methodist Church of the South Georgia Conference Archives; Clermont H. Lee; June McCash; Joe McDonough; Beau Sam McGowan; Jack McKinney; Peggy McMath; Nathalee McNeely; Walter McNeely; Scotty McPhee; Gov. Lester Maddox; Alfred Martin; Dot Mason; Joe Mason; Marvin Massey; Gertrude Maxwell; Laurence Miller Jr.; Wesley Millican; Bill Minter; Eric Moody; Yank Moore; Sandra Mungin; Lyneath Musgrove; Beverly Myers; Bill Newberry; Mary Newberry; Ann North; Jerry North; Myrtle Oxford; O.V. Ottwell; Linda Dykes Pageant; Wallace Pageant; Caesar Pavia; Beth Peek; Marshall Peek; Tommy Penn; Kenneth Picha; Vivien Picha; Eddie Pickett; Louise Pippen; Len Polezak and the Fiore Sculpture and Art Center; Murray Poole; Pete Poole; Alfonza Ramsey; Louise Ringel; Michael Rose and the Atlanta History Center; Nadine Rush; Elizabeth Scarboro; Sam Scarboro; Judge Robert Scoggin; Martha Scoggin; Leona Scott; Tallu Fish Scott; Pat Shaw and the Church of God; Diann Silvernail; Calvin Sinnette; Hoke Gilbert Smith; Linda Smith; Sam Snead; Joe Spaulding; Donna Stewart and the Jekyll Island 4-H Center; Carmen Stovall; Sen. Herman Talmadge; Linda Talmadge; Lucy Thompson; Mildred Tichnell; Dena Torkildson; F.H. Torkildson; Billy Townsend and the Georgia State Parks Department; Gov. Ernest Vandiver; Leonardo Velazquez; Sami Walker; Mike Wamock; Wesley Wellman; Don West; Diane Wilkes; Jim Wilkes; Clyde Williams; B.J. Wilson; Jackie Yeomans; and Harold Zell.

Finally, appreciation goes to Katie White for her assistance and patience.